KINTSUGI

Robert D. Grappel

Kintsugi © 2025 Robert Grappel

ISBN 978-1-968970-45-1 (Paperback)
ISBN 978-1-968970-46-8 (Ebook)

Inquiries and Book Orders should be addressed to:

Leavitt Peak Press
17901 Pioneer Blvd Ste L #298, Artesia, California 90701
Phone #: 2092191548

Introduction

This is my third book of original poetry. My first book, GIFTS, was published eighteen years ago in 2007. My second one, REGIFTS, was published nine years ago in 2016. As I said then, I seldom (if ever) sit down to write a poem intentionally. Poems come to me out of the blue – like presents in the mail from far-off friends. I can edit and polish them, rewrapping and refining the original idea, but the real source of the inspiration is always a mysterious gift. Sometimes it comes from interactions with friends and family, other times from my religious or musical families. Sometimes it comes during trips to far-off places, and other times during quiet moments. In this book I pass along these gifts to you. I hope you enjoy them.

Biography

My journey to becoming a "serious" poet began during my freshman year in college at the University of Michigan. All of us "science nerds" were required to take at least one semester's credit of English to graduate. I was dead set that I would not waste my time in any freshman English course. Fortunately, the U. of M. honors college had a special program that would let a student take any course that was offered so long as the professor would accept you. I had dabbled with writing folk songs and parodies in high school, but with extreme nerve, I decided to sign up for a graduate-level course in poetry composition to satisfy my English requirement. I'm not sure why Professor Hall accepted me into his course, but I can tell you that his class was the hardest 'B' I've ever obtained in college – it made freshman Physics seem easy by comparison.

Professor Hall required that we each write a new poem for each class. He also wrote a new poem for each class. All the poems were read aloud in class anonymously, and the discussion/critiques that followed were often quite spirited. Even Professor Hall's poems did not escape the class's criticism. (Two years later, I had Professor Hall's son in a Physics class where I was the teaching assistant – I had to restrain my criticism of his work.)

Professor Donald Hall was the author of over 50 books across several genres from children's literature, biography, memoir, essays, and including 22 volumes of verse. He was the 14th Poet Laureate of the United States.

In most bookstores, poetry books are shelved alphabetically by the author's name. My three thin volumes of original poetry are right there next to Donald Hall's many books. I wonder if he knew what he had started when he let a freshman enroll in his class in 1968.

Acknowledgements

This book contains quite a bit beyond poetry. The author would like to thank Ivan Stiles and Christiana Wamsley for their illustrations of many of the poems.

I wish to thank Ramona Pina of "Book Baby" for her help in shepherding this book to its finished form".

The author's photograph is by *Picture People.*

The cover photograph "Bowels of the Earth – Water" is gratefully used with permission of the artist, Naoko Fukumaru.

Naoko Fukumaru was born in Japan to a third-generation antique dealer. Her family's auction-house family was started by her great-grandfather, who collected by wheelbarrow unwanted broken objects which he restored and sold. Her father regularly brought home damaged, abandoned ceramics from his auction house. Every day, they ate from beautiful antique plates that were cracked or chipped, her baby food from imperfect old Imari porcelain. Later, Fukumaru studied ceramic conservation in England, focusing on Western "hidden" restoration practices. She has worked for over two decades as a professional ceramic and glass conservator at the Detroit Institute of Arts Museum, the Metropolitan Museum of Art New York, and other institutions in the USA, Europe, Egypt, and Japan. She has also worked for artists Anish Kapoor, Yoko Ono, and Peter Greenaway. She now applies her expertise and skills to Kintsugi. But, instead of hiding imperfections, she creatively celebrates them. Fukumaru's artwork aims to open people and to encourage self-acceptance, to help heal ourselves and the world. Suffering and flaws are integral parts of our identity, elements that shape our history and uniqueness. By beautifully magnifying imperfections in objects, her work allows us to accept fragility and imperfection in ourselves and in life. By celebrating imperfection and impermanence in life she explores what it means to be beautifully broken.

The Cover

The cover of this book illustrates the poem "Kintsugi". This poem was inspired when I watched a television story about this ancient Japanese art form.

Kintsugi (金継ぎ, "golden joinery"), also known as Kintsukuroi (金繕い, "golden repair"), is the Japanese art of repairing broken pottery by mending the areas of breakage with lacquer dusted or mixed with powdered gold, silver, or platinum, a method simi- lar to 'Maki-e' technique. As a philosophy it treats breakage and repair as part of the history of an object, rather than something to disguise.

Kintsugi became closely associated with ceramic vessels used for 'chanoyu' (Japanese tea ceremony). One theory is that kintsugi may have origi- nated when Japanese shogun Ashikaga Yoshimasa sent a damaged Chinese tea bowl back to China for repairs in the late 15th century. When it was returned, repaired with ugly metal staples, it may have prompted Japanese craftsmen to look for a more aesthetic means of repair. Collectors became so enamored of the new art that some were accused of deliber- ately smashing valuable pottery so it could be repaired with the golden seams of kintsugi.

無心Kintsugi can relate to the Japanese philosophy of "no mind" (mushin), which encompasses the con- cepts of non-attachment, acceptance of change, and fate as aspects of human life.

"Not only is there no attempt to hide the damage, and the repair is literally illuminated... a kind of physical expression of the spirit of 'mushin'. 'Mushin'

is often literally translated as "no mind," but carries connotations of fully existing within the moment, of non-attachment, of equanimity amid changing conditions.

...The vicissitudes of existence over time, to which all humans are susceptible, could not be clearer than in the breaks, the knocks, and the shattering to which ceramic ware too is subject. This poignancy or aesthetic of existence has been known in Japan as mono no aware, a compassionate sensitivity, or perhaps identi-fication with, [things] outside oneself. "

—Christy Bartlett, Flickwerk: "The Aesthetics of Mended Japanese Ceramics"

Ivan Stiles

A Federation of Planets

I've been a 'Trekkie' ever since the original version of the show was first broadcast way back in 1966. Star Trek's brightly optimistic worldview of humanity in the 24th century has always been very appealing to me. This optimism becomes ever more appealing in today's increasingly polarized world.

A dashing young captain from Iowa
Portrayed by a Canadian from Montreal (Kirk/Shatner).

A balding, older captain from La Barre, France,
Portrayed by a Shakespearean actor
Who speaks with an English accent (Picard/Stewart).

A woman captain voyaging the Delta Quadrant
While actually born in Iowa (Janeway/Mulgrew).

A half-Vulcan Science Officer,
Who was a Jewish boy from Boston (Spock/Nimoy).

An android First Officer – built, not born,
Who was a Jewish boy from Houston (Data/Spiner).

A tall First-Officer from Alaska,
Who was actually born in central Pennsylvania (Riker/Frakes).

A Scottish Chief Engineer who likes his whiskey,
Born to Irish parents in Vancouver, Canada,
And fought at Normandy on D-Day (Scotty/Doohan).

A blind Chief Engineer and Helmsman,
Born in West Germany,
And starred in "Roots" (Geordi/Burton).

A communications officer from Africa,
Her Swahili name means "freedom",
Was a jazz singer from Chicago (Uhuru/Nichols).

A Chief Helmsman born in San Francisco
To Japanese-American parents in both centuries,
And interned in a prison camp during WWII (Sulu/Takei).

The Chief of Security and later a Romulan Commander
Who was really born in Hollywood (Yar/Crosby).

The first ship's doctor with a southern accent
Actually was born in Georgia,
And really wanted to be a doctor (McCoy/Kelley).

The second ship's doctor was a woman, born on the moon,
With flaming red hair and Scottish parents.
She was really born in Ohio,
And has Lithuanian parents (Crusher/Mc Fadden).

A black, half-Klingon orphan raised by humans,
With a half-human wife and a clouded heritage,
Became acting Security Chief when Tasha Yar died (Worf/Dorn).

A half-Betazoid ship's Counselor,
Was born in London to Greek parents (Troi/Sirtis).

A Russian-born ship's Navigator
And a young face from Chicago (Chekov/Koenig).

Another young face as acting Ensign,
Son of Federation Officers,
Whose inner talents only become apparent much later,
And was a native Californian (Crusher/Wheaton).

Not exactly a melting pot of races,
More like a federation of planets.

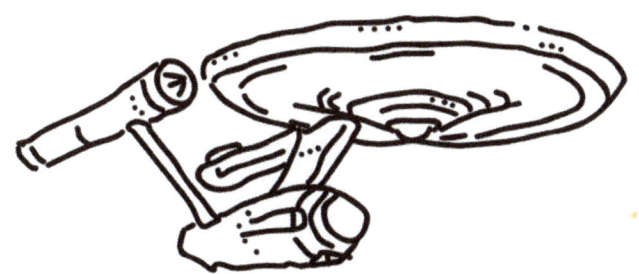

Ivan Stiles

Christiana Wamsley

A Modern Bill of Rights

(1)   I have the right to be ignorant.
      In a world where knowledge is readily available,
      Free and at my fingertips day and night,
      More than at any other time in history,
      I can just choose to ignore it.

(2)   I have the right to disseminate my ignorance.
      I don't need to check my 'facts'.
      I don't need to think critically about my deductions.
      I can broadcast my raw lack of information
      To anyone who might care to listen.

(3)   I have the right to be stubborn.
      When the world does not adhere to my beliefs,
      And events do not evolve according to my wishes,
      I can simply choose to ignore any evidence I don't like.

(4)   I have the right to demand equality
      For my uneducated ideas.
      What I read on my favorite Internet site
      Should stand side-by-side with
      The views of life-long experts.
      I don't need to learn anything new
      Or consider any opposing views.

(5)   I have the right to hold tightly to my prejudices.
      "My country, right or wrong."
      My group is entitled to the best of everything.
      When I help another, it lessens me.
      Charity is a sign of weakness.

I am fortunate to live where I have these 'rights'.
I am also fortunate enough not to express them.
I have the opportunity to learn and grow.
This is my most important right.

Christiana Wamsley

An African Proverb

An African proverb relates that
"When an old man dies,
A library burns down".
This poet is an old man.

History section
First-hand memories of events and times
Recollections of the past
And dreams left for others

Sociology section
Stories of friends and family
Lives shared and touched
And regrets of opportunities missed

Travel section
Photo albums and videos
Tours taken and sights seen
And items left on the "bucket list"

Science section
Experiments tried and failed
Some successes, a few near misses
And many enigmas left to explore.

Biography section
One fewer volume on the shelves.

Ivan Stiles

An Old Funny Story

This poem is based on an old funny story involving a flood, a helicopter, and one or more boats. The 'punch line' has stayed the same, even though the build-up is a bit different.

It was the time of pandemic,
And a man of fervent faith was quarantined at home.
Each night, he prayed to God
"Please keep my family safe and healthy".

Next day, God had the State Governor give a speech.
There were health officials
And the local football coach,
Each telling the man to wash his hands,
To avoid large social gatherings,
Where to obtain disinfecting supplies,
And other basic precautions.
"These things will help keep you safe and healthy",
Said the Governor.

The man shouted back at his TV,
"God will protect me and my family!",
And he prayed again.

The next day, the Mayor shut down the city.
She gave a press conference,
Echoing the advice of the health officials
And the State Governor.
All day long the news broadcast advice
And precautions to take,
How to avoid the spread of the virus,
And why 'social-distancing' was important.
Again, that night, the man prayed.

The next morning, the man watched news reports
With scientists giving the same advice,
And there was a special report by the President
Describing his plan to distribute vaccines.

It was the weekend now.
Still the man said, "I'm praying to God,
And He is going to save me and my family.
I have faith."

The man took his entire family to church
On Sunday morning.
They had a fine meal at their favorite restaurant.
On the radio, they heard public officials
Urging everyone to stay home.
Their preacher told them God would keep them safe,
If only they would "trust in the Lord."
They all felt very good.
"It's just like the flu", he said,
"And God will care for us."

A couple of days passed, and the man began feeling ill.
He was diagnosed with Covid-19, sickened, and died.
He went to Heaven.

He got his chance to discuss this situation with God.
The man exclaimed,
"I had faith in You, but You didn't save me!
You let me die!
I just don't understand why!"

God replied,
"I sent you a President, a Governor, a Mayor,
Doctors, Nurses, Health officials,
Radio and television personalities,
Even friends on Facebook.
What more did you expect?
What else did you want?"

The man then asked,
"Who are these people behind me?"
God replied, "those are the other people who died
Because you disregarded the advice I sent you".

Christiana Wamsley

Ivan Stiles

A Groove Or A Rut

This poem was suggested by a discussion I had with Lucille Reilly at the Northwest Autoharp Gathering (NWAG) on how so many autoharp play- ers (myself included) get into bad habits that keep them from prog- ress- ing beyond a certain point.

When does a groove
Become a rut?
I'm lazy
And crazy,
But…

I do enjoy safety,
But somehow lately,
I feel that just maybe,
That groove isn't quite
Wide enough.

Ivan Stiles

A Pleasant Walk on the Beach

This poem was inspired during our MLAG 2017 cruise tour of the Omaha and Utah beaches in Normandy, France. It was hard to imagine the awful things that happened here 73 years ago. It seemed more like a pictur- esque site for a picnic by the sea than a place of horror and death for many thousands.

We stepped down from our comfortable bus,
Strong winds whipping the flags to attention.
We walked across the parking lot
And along a narrow path towards the sea,
Just a quiet group of tourists,
Only the crunch of shoes on gravel,
On a cool spring day.

Grassy mounds lie as far as the eye can see
Remains of shell craters not yet erased
By years of wind and rain,
The marching of visitors' feet,
And the passing of the years.

Concrete bunkers still stand watch out to sea
Skeletal tangles of rusted steel reinforcements
With here and there a bullet hole,
Awaiting their eventual demise,
When the constant sea erodes their foundations,
And they fall away before the waves' invasion.

This was the last sight for so many,
Germans looking out across the rocky beach,
And Allied soldiers staring in fear
Towards where we now stand
With our cameras and cellphones.
Too many graves, marked and not
Hallow this ground.

So, let us never forget
The heavy price that was paid
For our pleasant walk
On this beach.

Ivan Stiles

Christiana Wamsley

A Trash Compactor In Heaven

When I imagine Heaven, I think about a warm, sunny day
With trees and flowers everywhere I look,
Bright greens and the scent of blossoms,
A tranquil pool and splashing fountains.
The only noises are the calls of birds.
I get to live in such a place. It's called 'Toscana'.

They plan to build a trash compactor
Across the parking lot
In front of my paradise.
Mechanical noises and garbage trucks will drive
Through my image of heaven
I guess that it's a necessary evil.
Even the Garden of Eden had snakes.

All of us living here do generate trash
That must be hauled away somehow.
Even heaven must have a dumpster
Where the fallen leaves and uneaten fruits go.
To quote Arlo of "Alice's Restaurant"
"One big pile is better than two little piles".
But why does the compactor have to rise
Where my view used to be?

I guess that even the roses in Paradise
Have thorns.

Ivan Stiles

Christiana Wamsley

Alvy's Error

In a flashback scene from the 1977 film "Annie Hall", Woody Allen's char- acter, Alvy Singer, is a depressed young boy who won't do his homework because, as he explains to his doctor: "The universe is expanding... Well, the universe is everything, and if it's expanding, someday it will break apart and that will be the end of everything." His exasperated mother upbraids him: "What has the universe to do with it? You're here in Brooklyn. Brooklyn is not expanding!"

It's all a matter of time-scale.
To the cosmos, each star flickers and is gone.
To the star, planets are just a phase in its life.
To a planet, life occupies but a moment.
But that moment is all we have to work with.

Will I do something great to change the world?
Probably not.
Will I change the course of history?
Not very likely.
Can I leave a mark on the sands of time?
Yes, on each life that I touch along the way.

I must keep my personal time-scale short enough
Within the realm of the possible.
So that each day provides a reasonable opportunity for good.
When 'today' is all you have.

I should strive to keep my world ever expanding.
My range of friends, experiences, and dreams
Need encompass far more than my backyard.
It's all a matter of scale.

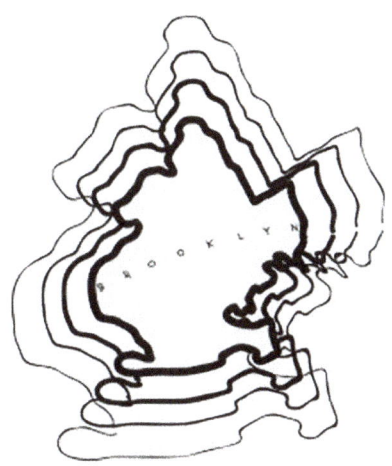

Ivan Stiles

Christiana Wamsley

As Simple As Black and White

The people of Jemez Pueblo came to these mesas about 1300 AD.
There they raised the craft of making pottery
From a utilitarian need,
A way to carry water and corn,
To a high art form.
White clay drawn from 'Mother Earth' in the New Mexican hills
And black decoration made from crushed lava rocks,
Beautiful examples of Jemez Black and White pottery
Now fill the shelves of museums and tourist shops.

In the mid 18th century, the Spanish came to these lands
To enslave and convert the native people.
The people of Jemez shattered their pottery
Pieces by the hundreds
To keep them from the hands of the greedy Spanish,
And they forgot how to make the ancient-style pots
For 200 years.

Today, the Jemez people have rediscovered their old techniques
And their ceramic artwork is now prized worldwide.
Jemez Black and White pottery is no longer
Just dusty relics in a museum,
But stand out as distinctive art.
Black and White is not always simple.

Ivan Stiles

As Simple As Day And Night

During the High Holidays, we are taught to pray
"God, grant us the ability to distinguish day from night".
What's the big deal about day and night?
Day is light and dark is night
Repeating in monotonous repetition.
Why a distinction worthy of our prayer?

In all my memory, day has followed night.
Throughout recorded history, day and night have alternated.
Was it always so?
Can we conceive of an endless stream
Of days and nights,
With no beginning and no ending,
Or, was there some wondrous burst of light
On that day of first creation,
And who was the Creator?

Daytime holds the bright sunshine,
With brilliant colors to delight us,
Illumination to guide our steps along the way.
Nighttime brings us the moon and stars
To remind us of worlds beyond our own.

But... what if we could not see the light and dark?
What if we were blind to daytime colors and nighttime stars?
We could still feel the warmth of daytime sun,
Hear sweet songs of birds awakening to greet the dawn,
Smell the scent of flowers rising in the air,
Feel the hush of evening twilight,
Know the peace of a gentle nighttime breeze,
The feel of soft sheets on a comfy bed,
And realize just how wonderful is the world
That has such beauty in it.

Most of us do our work in the daytime.
We earn our bread in the light of day,
Follow our dreams and perform our worthy deeds.
At night we rest and restore our souls
So the next day can bring productivity and joy.
We need to know how to separate
The day and its striving,
The night and its rebuilding.
We need the darkness to frame the light.

God, grant me the ability to distinguish day from night.

Ivan Stiles

Christiana Wamsley

Between a Rock and a Hard Place

This poem was inspired during a tour of Fort Lauderdale, Florida.

General Andrew Jackson led his army south into the Everglades.
It was 1817, and the first Seminole War was underway.
The Seminoles provided a safe haven for escaped slaves
And the southern states lusted after room to expand.
The war ended in a stalemate, but
Twelve years later, Jackson won the presidency
Appealing to the "common man".
Apparently, Indians and Negroes didn't qualify
As "men".

In 1835, the Seminoles refused to relocate to a reservation
Far from their native lands and Lake Okeechobee.
This began the second Seminole War.
The longest war between the United States and an Indian nation
Lasted seven years and multiple U.S. generals met defeat.
Finally, U.S. General Jessup captured the Seminole chiefs
Under a false flag of truce.

The second Seminole War ended
With no peace treaty or armistice.
More than 1,500 U.S. soldiers had died,
And the cost was 15 million dollars.
A handful of Seminoles – less than 500 –
Were left to die out deep in the Florida Everglades.

In 1855, the third Seminole War began
As a series of skirmishes over land ownership.
Three years later, Chief Billy Bowlegs

Lead most of the remaining Seminoles out of Florida,
While a small band remained hidden
In the Big Cypress Swamp.

Flash forward more than one and a half centuries.
The Seminole "Hard Rock" Hotel rises
Above the skyline of Fort Lauderdale.
With almost 1,300 luxury rooms
In a guitar-shaped building
That could house the entire 1858 tribe in total luxury.

The ultimate symbol of "rock-and-roll",
The music of rebellion against authority.
I guess the Seminoles did eventually win the battle.

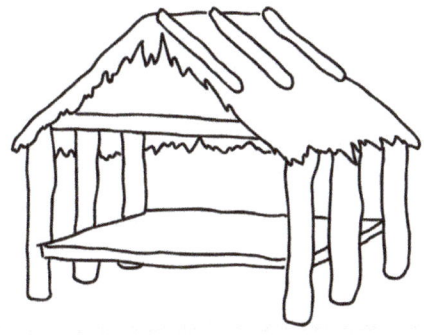

Ivan Stiles

Christiana Wamsley

Bloom Where You're Planted

Thanks to Edwina Goodhue who told me about the sunflower that she saw growing out of the rain gutter at her house.

A small speckled bird swallowed this sunflower seed
That lay in the leaf-litter along the garden's edge.
She flew up to perch along my roof eave
And sang her songs of joy to the noonday sun.

Time passed…
And this seed fell on the shingles
Then rolled unnoticed into my rain gutter.
More time passed…warm sun and gentle rain…
Nestled among the pine needles
And last-year's leaves.

Until, one day, the miracle of life began anew.
That seed drew sustenance from decay and light
And sprouted – peeking up over the gutter edge
To raise its head and salute the day.

I praise the song of that speckled bird.
I praise the tenacity of that sunflower seed.
Marking a miracle
Where others see just happy accident
We need only to look around.

It may lie dormant under a dead leaf,
Or just over our heads, singing.
Life's wondrous cycles are everywhere
If we only just look around.

Ivan Stiles

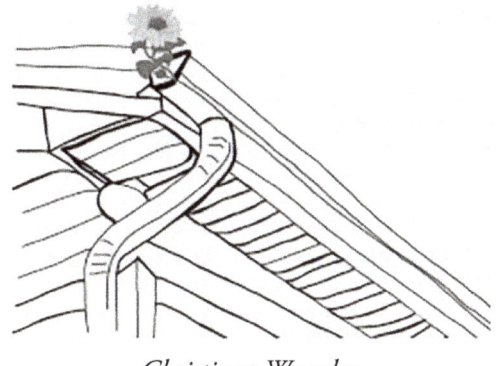

Christiana Wamsley

Deuteronomy 26:5

These three verses from the Bible form the core of the Passover Seder observance. They are still meaningful millennia later.

My father was a fugitive Aramean.
>   In Biblical times,
>   'Aram' was an obscure corner of Canaan.
>   Later, it was a village in Poland,
>   A ghetto in the Ukraine,
>   Uganda, Cuba, Curacao,
>   Towns across the Soviet Union,
>   Every place where people seek freedom.
>   We remember as though we live there ourselves.
>   No one can assume liberty as their right.

He went down to Egypt with meager numbers and sojourned there.
>   We travel throughout our lives,
>   From the places of our childhood,
>   To our final resting places.
>   We journey within a small community
>   Of family and friends.
>   No place inherently 'ours',
>   We share this world with all our fellow travelers.

There he became a great and very populous nation.
>   The Bible's wording is not redundant here.
>   A large population does not make a nation 'great'.
>   A strong economy or a powerful army
>   Need not lead a people to greatness.
>   True greatness must come in what we pick up
>   Along the road from 'Aram' to 'home'.

Don't Raise the Bridge – Lower the River

This poem was written just after the tragic shooting to death of 17 people at a school in Parkland, Florida. President Trump proposed that the solution to preventing such tragedies in the future was to issue guns to teachers.

You have a gun
That makes me feel afraid.
Now I have a gun
And it's twice as likely that someone will get shot.
You tell me that I should feel more comfortable now.
I just don't see the logic.

You don't have a gun
And I don't have a gun.
There's no chance that someone will be shot.
This, I can understand.

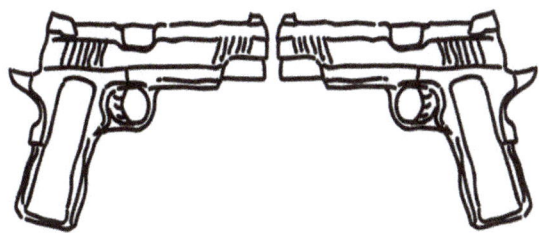

Ivan Stiles

Dunbar Circles

The Oxford evolutionary psychologist Robin Dunbar is best known for his namesake "Dunbar's number," which he defines as the number of stable relationships people are cognitively able to maintain at once. (The proposed number is 150.) But after spending his decades-long career studying the complexities of friendship, he's discovered many more numbers that shape our close relationships. He's also studied the seven factors that people use to evaluate whether someone has the potential to become a friend, and the average number of hours it takes for an acquaintance to become a close friend.

I'm an only child
My inner circle is one.
My wife, Lynda, is my intimate
And maybe my cat counts there too.

Three times larger is my "shoulders to cry on" circle.
Who'll drop everything when I reach out.
Three times larger includes shared 'fun times' people.
I'd trust them with my valued possessions.

The next layer out is my 'weekend-barbecue' people.
And the 150 layer is my weddings and funerals group
Who would come to a once-in-a-lifetime event.

Dunbar layers form because
Our time for social interaction is not infinite.
I must decide how to invest that time,
Bearing in mind that the strength of my relationships
Directly correlates to how much time and effort
I choose to give them.

Introverts like me are risk averse.
We 'd prefer to have fewer friends,
So, we can invest more time in each.

Extroverts are more socially confident.
They prefer to have more friends
At the cost of investing less time in each.
They feel that they can wing it with someone else.
If one friend says no.
These are just two equally good ways
Of solving the same problem.

Who are your friends changes constantly.
You don't throw away all your friends and start again.
There's this kind of churning going on.
When you're younger, late teens and early 20s,
The churn rate can be very high indeed.
Losing and gaining
A consequence of who you're exposed to.
Have I moved to a new place for school or a new job?
Have I just been exposed to a new group of people?
That stabilizes by about the 30s, in most cases,
Because babies are the killer for any kind of social life
For everyone.
But the number starts to decline into old age
By virtue of progressively losing the outermost layers
It ends up, if you live long enough,
With just the innermost layer of 1.5.

If you meet a new person, fall in love, and get married,
You're investing a lot of time and mental energy
In that relationship.
You essentially have to sacrifice two people.
You meet this new person,
Now you now have six in your inner circle,
So, somebody has to go.
But the new person takes up to two rations of time.
So, you end up losing two people, who drop into the next circle,
Who push two people from that circle out
Into the third circle. It's a domino effect.

There are "seven pillars of friendship"
That people use to evaluate
How likely it is
That they will become your friends.
They are seven dimensions of who you are
That form the basis of friendship.
It is the tendency for like to associate with like.
"Birds of a feather flock together."
Our friends are very similar to us.
Sharing the same language,
Growing up in the same location,
Having similar worldviews
Moral, religious, and political.
Having the same sense of humor.
Having the same musical taste.

The seven pillars are substitutable
Each is as good as any other.
A three-pillar friendship can form
With any combination.
Liking the same music seems to be especially good.

It takes about 200 hours of investment
In the space of a few months
To move a stranger into being a good friend.
Close friends are very expensive
In time invested to maintain them.
I think these figures are a guideline – not precise.
It just means that friendships require work.

So, don't be too afraid to lose a friend.
It might be a healthy pruning.
Don't be fazed by the loss of friends.
It's an opportunity to go off and make new friends,
Who may turn out to be even better.

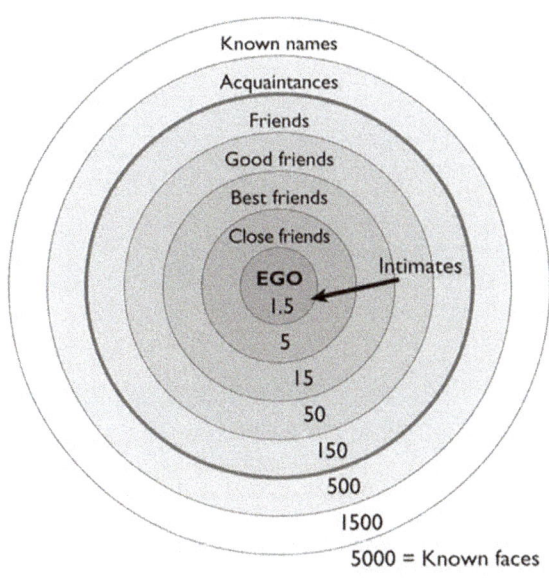

Expensive Tiles

Lynda and I went to the tile store today.
We were looking for a new condo floor
Porcelain, 18 inches square,
Matte finish, gray-streaked marble-style.

So expensive
For something made from dirt.
Porcelain is but baked clay
And glass is just fired sand.
The colors come from smelted metallic ores.
The art is in the mixing and combining.

People are like these tiles.
The Bible says that we were made from dust.
We end as dust too.
Our value is in the combinations
And the mixing,
The multitude of patterns and finishes,
And the colors.

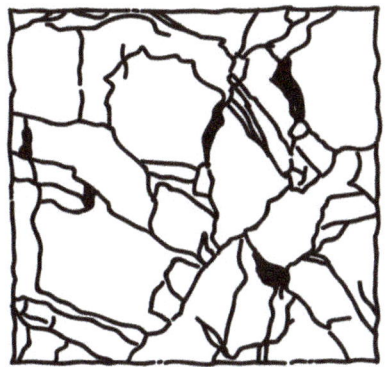

Ivan Stiles

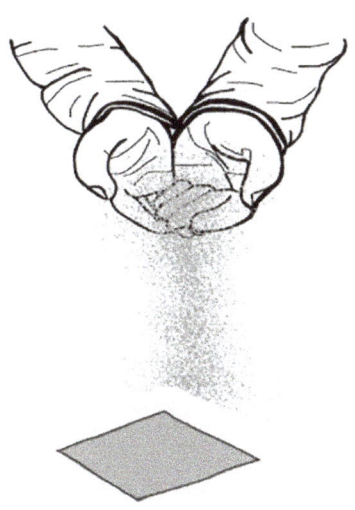

Christiana Wamsley

Extinction Burst

"An <u>extinction burst</u> is a concept from behavioral psychology. It involves the idea of eliminating an undesirable behavior by refusing to rein- force it.

The best example of this is a child's tantrum. Parents react to tantrums, which is why they often work, but the point of the tantrum is primarily **attention**. *So when the parent reacts, it reinforces the tantrum and increases the frequency of it. What many parents fail to understand is that even a spanking or yelling is still attention and still helps to reinforce the tantrum.*

What is generally very effective about reducing tantrums is not attention, but a complete dearth of it. As difficult as it is to do so, the tantrum will generally go away once the attention is removed. But first there is the extinction burst. "

Thanks to Cathy Beyer, who introduced me to the extinction burst concept. In this poem, I've taken the term far from its psychological roots — but I claim that this is a poet's right.

No, this poem's not about dinosaurs.
Well, maybe it is to some degree
For without the extinction event that ended the age of reptiles
And allowed mammals to flourish and evolve
It's not likely I'd be here to write this poem.

Around 1900, Lord Kelvin is supposed to have said:
"There is nothing new to be discovered in physics now.
All that remains is more and more precise measurement."
In ten short years, relativity and quantum mechanics
Swept away all those old foundations.

When I first learned astronomy there were nine planets
One unique solar system, alone in a starry heaven.
With precise measurements
Today we know thousands of planets
Each with the possibility of life
Looking back towards that common star
That I call home.

When I first learned physics there were just matter and energy.
Not simple things, but comprehensible at least.
A few unexplained gravitational measurements in the cosmos.
New concepts like "dark matter" and "dark energy"
Show us today that we don't know the 'half of it'.

I'm sure that the luxury coach builders in the 1900's
Struggled to understand the appeal of those noisy,
Smelly first automobiles
Clattering along rutted streets and scaring the horses,
Yet, if Henry Ford had known about lithium-ion batteries
Instead of gasoline engines,
We'd all be driving Teslas today.

Today, the coal business is facing its own "extinction burst"
A struggle to realize that the world must move on.
We can change or choke to death – what seems an easy choice.
Dramatic change is almost always scary.
Sometimes trying to extend the known into the future
Just won't work.
Ask the buggy-whip makers of 1910.

This poet will retire in September.
Fifty years at one career.
I can rail against the necessary changes
Throw a tantrum, and hold my breath.
But I hope to see this as a new beginning
Opening to a bright new day.

Ivan Stiles

Feynman's Formula

The Nobel Prize-winning physicist, Richard Feynman, understood the difference between "knowing something" and "knowing the name of something". He felt that this was one of the most important reasons for his success. Feynman developed a 'formula for learning' that ensured he understood certain things better than almost anyone else. His formula works for any concept, subject, or topic that you might want to learn, and it has just four simple steps.

(1) **Teach it to a child**
   The Bible relates,
   "You shall teach these words to your children".
   It's not only the children who do the learning.
   The teacher gains as much from replying to the questions
   As the student gleans from the answers,
   And there'll be many more
   Than just the Seder's set of four.
   Don't blindly recite the words and follow the forms.
   These are just the names of the things
   You want to learn.

(2) **Review**
   What seemed true to a teenage Bar Mitzvah student
   Appears far differently to a 30-something
   With children of his own.
   My grandparents experienced
   An alternate reality from mine.
   What seemed clear in a middle-ages European ghetto
   Might be viewed quite differently
   In today's 'global village'.
   We must seek the constants that do not change.
   We should strive to fill the gaps in our knowledge.
   True competence comes from knowing
   The limits of our abilities.

(3) **Organize and Simplify**
Every year or so, review your subject notes.
Read them out loud.
If it doesn't sound convincing to you.
If the story doesn't quite ring true,
Maybe your understanding still needs some work.
The Bible stories and the histories
Need further clarification and elaboration.
As each year we come to them
With new minds and hearts.

(4) **Transmit**
The Bible goes on to say,
"You shall speak of these words at home and away,
Morning and evening."
The ultimate test of one's knowledge lies
In the capacity to convey it to another.
We're all children in one subject or another,
Each capable of teaching and desirous of learning.
The person who says that he knows what he thinks
But cannot express it to another
Does not know what he really thinks.

Finding Happiness

A teacher once gave each of his students a balloon.
He said, "Blow up your balloon.
Write your name on it.
Then throw it out into the hallway".

The teacher then mixed up all the balloons, and said:
"You now have five minutes to find your own balloon".

A frantic search ensued, but no student could find their balloon.

The teacher then said, "Try this approach instead.
Take the first balloon you can find in the hallway,
Read the name written on it,
And hand it back to that person".

Within five minutes, every student had their own balloon.

These balloons are like happiness.
If you only look for your own, you might never find it.
If you look for the happiness of others
You will find your own as well.

Ivan Stiles

Fire and Snow

Imagine a pillar of fire
Two miles high and more
Glowing, white-hot, liquid rock
Extending upwards from the core
In the Cascade Range of northern Oregon.

Imagine a skiers' paradise
Year-round powder snowfields
Shining white against the mountainside
Where ski lifts reach upward towards glaciers
And sights of neon-colored parkas dot the higher trails.

Now, imagine these both together,
A vibrant ski scene and a hiking mecca,
Timberline Lodge, luxury and old-world artistry,
Forests green, glistening snow, and rocky majesty
Join to form the majestic pyramid that is Mount Hood.

Ivan Stiles

Christiana Wamsley

Foams

Some of the best things in the world
Are foams.
Suds on a pitcher of beer,
Froth left on a sandy beach just after a wave breaks,
Steamed milk on a cappuccino,
Meringue on a pie,
A bath sponge,
Wood,
A pool noodle,
A pillow,
And whipped cream.

In this year of COVID,
We are each encased in our socially-distanced bubbles.
We need to remember that…
Taken together…
We form a foam of humanity…
A beautiful thing.

Ivan Stiles

Christiana Wamsley

Four States of Consciousness

In his science fiction novel "Earth", David Brin writes about the four ways that people may react to experiencing a new situation.

Aha
Wow, this is great!
I wonder what else it can do.
I'm so curious…
I want to look further…
I'm so excited!

Ho-hum
Yeah, yeah, really great.
Just another 'new thing'.
You can have it if you want.
I'm OK with what I have already.
Who needs anything else?

Oy-vey
This thing is scary.
It's going to upset things.
Changes frighten me.
They always cause trouble.
My life was fine before.

Yum-yum
This satiates my senses.
I want to consume more and more.
I need a lot of it,
More than anyone else.
They can't have any of mine!

From the Mountain

The last two chapters in the book of Leviticus in the Bible contain what seem to be a really odd (to this poet) collection of legal regulations and commandments for the people of Israel who are still camped out in the desert at the foot of Mt. Sinai. What is even stranger is how these rules can have any meaning for me today. This poem is my attempt to sort it out.

The Sabbatical Year

We're to let all the farmland rest every seventh year.
OK, so crop rotation is a good thing.
Nature needs recovery time, just like people do.
But…I'm not a farmer.
I get my food from a store
And eat at restaurants.
What does the Sabbatical Year have to do with me?

Maybe we're to treat the land as our partner in creation.
Good things are not just the result of our own labor.
So, just like our farmhands and ourselves,
Nature deserves its time of rest.
A Sabbath to remind us of the world around
And what remains yet to be done
For the poor and the hungry
Tomorrow.

The Jubilee Year

Every fiftieth year all slaves shall go free.
But…I don't own any slaves.
Slavery ended long ago.
What does this Jubilee have to do with me?

Many people today live under crushing debts.
Unable to live free and be all they could be,
They might as well be slaves.
Poverty can be a form of enslavement.
Generation after generation
Longing for the standard of life
That I take for granted.

Every fiftieth year all land reverts to its original owner.
Wealth should not separate people into layers.
'Haves' and 'have-nots'
Should not be a permanent condition.
Once a generation (every fifty years or so)
We should all receive a "get out of jail free" card.

You shall make no idols

Chapter 26 switches gears with a wrench.
After pages of rules for farming,
Ownership of land and slavery,
We're told not to make idols,
Graven images,
Or pillars in the land.

Money can be an idol.
When it becomes an end rather than simply a tool.
A "graven image" could be a pile of "dead presidents"
Or an art collection.
A "pillar in the land" might be an oversize mansion.
Or a wall to keep people out.

So…this stuff is important for me too.
Even if I'm not a farmer
Or a real estate developer.
Important enough to be told from the mountaintop
And remembered by all the people.
The opposite of poverty is not wealth,
It's justice.

Global Warming

Hot air…
We've got far too much of it
Rising from the un-drained swamps of Washington, DC.
Shortsighted thinkers must face long-term problems.
Masses of turbulent air
From the right and the left collide
With much thunder and lightning
But without a noticeable result.

Let's "make America great again".
Not by buying up Greenland
(There's not enough ice left there to cool the rhetoric!),
And not by burying our heads in aging coal mines
(They're not deep enough to stifle
The coughing sounds from above).

Rather – greatness derives from leadership
Looking forward boldly, not backward with nostalgia.
For when the winds of change
Start to blow loud and strong
It is better to raise a sail
And steer bravely towards the sunlit shore
Than to hide in a storm cellar.

Ivan Stiles

Christiana Wamsley

God's Business Card

Thank you, Rabbi Mike, for this wonderful and powerful image. Yes, I really was listening to your sermon yesterday.

Suppose that you wanted to build a new world.
You would need to hire a 'cosmic' contractor,
And an awesome architect,
And a landscaper with vivid imagination,
And you wanted the job completed in six working days.

Suppose that you want to renovate
A war-torn, ravaged world.
You'll need a careful carpenter
To repair the rotten beams
And patch the deteriorating wallboard,
And pour new foundations
Where the ground has shifted.
You'll require an electrician
To avoid a 'shocking' conclusion.

You'll want a master plumber
To keep the water pure and flowing.
You'll want an HVAC technician
To keep the air clean and at a comfortable temperature.
You'll want a good interior decorator
To stage the open house
For the next generation of buyers yet to come.
A certificate from the building inspector
Is another must.

Before you hire that contractor, plumber, or decorator
You'll want to see examples of their work.
You'll have to check their references.
Maybe scan their websites and read their reviews.
So…look up at the perfect blue dome
Of the sunlit sky at noon.
Watch the smooth curve of an ocean wave.
Enjoy the beauty of a hillside carpeted with wildflowers.
Smell the woodsy scent of a forest breeze.
Gaze at the stars on a winter's night.

So…let us all strive to live constructive lives
To write on the back
Of the Great Contractor's business card
"Good references!"

Ivan Stiles

Christiana Wamsley

Haecceity

This word stems from the medieval Latin "haecceitas." It comes from the Latin "haec," feminine of "hic," meaning "this."

Haecceity is a deeply philosophical concept attributed to Scottish Catholic priest and university professor John Duns Scotus. He defined it as a non-qualitative property of a substance or thing that is respon- sible for its individuation and identity, such as a particular person's unique iden- tity. Interestingly, Scotus is also where the term "dunces" originated from. His opponents equated Duns' followers, who argued against Renaissance humanism, to dullards incapable of scholarship.

I am not a Republican,
Although I've voted for their candidates once or twice.
I am not a Democrat either,
Although I've voted for them a time or more too.
I am not always a conservative
And I'm not always a liberal either.
I am a Jewish male white American
But none of these categories fully defines
Who I am.

I have been a "dog person" as a boy,
Now I love my cat too.
I respect tradition and established values
Yet I work to develop new technologies.
I have had a career in science and engineering,
But I'm also a poet and a musician.
I was born a natural left-hander
But I play my instruments righty.

I don't comfortably fit any one definition.
I'm just me.

Heterophony

*In music, **heterophony** is a type of texture characterized by the simultaneous variation of a single melodic line. Such a texture can be regarded as a kind of complex monophony in which there is only one basic melody, but realized at the same time in multiple voices, each of which plays the melody differently, either in a different rhythm or tempo, or with various embellishments and elaborations.*

All humanity sings the same song,
From start to finish,
From our birth to our death,
From key signature to the double bar.

Some sing faster with lots of vigor
Swinging the beat and changing the volume,
While others sing their song at a slower tempo
And with, perhaps, fewer repeats.

Some add personal variations to the tune
With melodic ornaments
While others sing the melody plain and simple
No extra notes or deviations.

There are local versions to the tune
Sometimes a minor chord intrudes.
Sometimes there's a syncopation,
A hold, a note cut short, or an extra rest.

The song we're singing is simply life.
One basic tune in infinite variation.
Each person makes the tune their own.
So, sing yours sweetly.

Ivan Stiles

Christiana Wamsley

Homeopathic Seder

Homeopathy is a medical system that was developed in Germany more than 200 years ago. This system is based on two unconventional theories:

- *"Like cures like"—the notion that a disease can be cured by a substance that produces similar symptoms in healthy people*
- *"Law of minimum dose"—the notion that the lower the dose of the medication, the greater its effectiveness. Many homeopathic products are so diluted that no molecules of the original substance remain.*

This poem was inspired by an invitation that my wife and I received to a "very, very, ultra-reform Seder – just the four questions, a few blessings, and a catered meal from a local deli". The invitation was 'BYOB'.

Take one dose of a therapeutic substance
That produces results for people
Who might not need curing.
Mix it with water,
Over and over and over,
Until nothing original remains
But the water
And the belief that this medicine will be effective.

Take a religious observance,
And centuries-old traditions.
Remove the poetry and familiar songs.
Leave out the ancient stories and ignore the history.
Nothing relevant to our lives today
But the food.

A few blessings
But no remembrance of to whom we are praying.
Four questions,
But no answers.

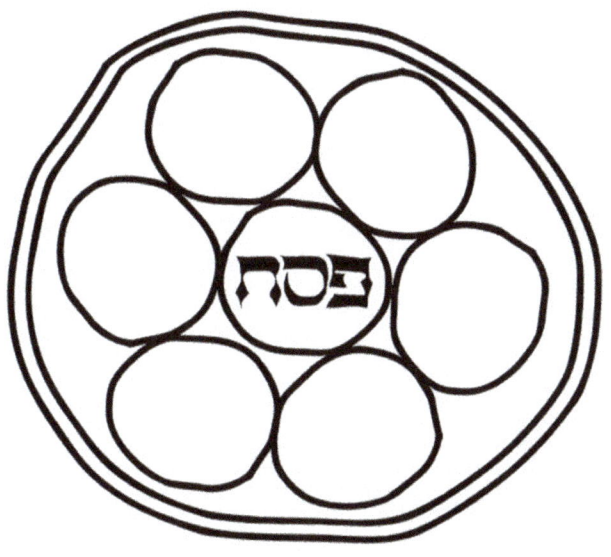

Ivan Stiles

How To See The Stars

Today's a bright, sunny day.
A bit too cold, perhaps,
And a bit too breezy,
But, taken all in all,
A pleasant time to be outside.

My heart is dark and clouded though.
I've lost too many loved ones,
Dear friends and joys no longer.
Sickness and frustrations
Cloud over my daylight sky.

My world is full of petty hatreds,
Reports of wars and shouts of discord.
The news is always blue and red,
Like a giant bruise,
Too painful to think about.

Yet, when the world is at its darkest,
When no background light intrudes,
That is when the sky is full of stars
When their unmatched beauty,
Shines to gladden even the darkest heart.

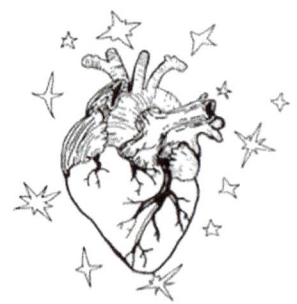

Christiana Wamsley

I Did Promise You a Rose Garden

This poem came to me during a tour of the International Rose Test Garden in Portland, Oregon. Nicknamed the "City of Roses", Portland has been the home since 1917 to a spectacular garden established to preserve European rose species that could have been lost due to the ravages of World War I. The garden has more than 7,000 rose plants of every color, shape, and size.

The poem's title (and some of the imagery) comes from the popular country song "I Never Promised You a Rose Garden" written by Joe South in 1969 and made a hit recording by Lynn Anderson in 1970.

On the third day of creation
God made all the flowering plants.
They were His first thoughts
After forming the Earth,
Even before the sun and stars,
And the Bible says
"God saw that it was good".

On the sixth day of creation
God turned over care of His world
To humanity
For its preservation,
And the Bible says
"God saw all that He had made
And it was very good".

Roses are incredibly diverse plants.
There are miniatures and teas,
Climbers and trees.
Every color of the spectrum represented
In petal whorls, bright in the sunlight.
Singles, doubles, and variegated.
They are each very beautiful.

Roses have sharp thorns for protection
And pleasing scents for attraction.
They thrive best in direct sun
But, contrary to the popular song,
Need lots of rain to flower.
All sides of nature in balance
Yielding a wondrous harmony.

So…we **were** promised a "rose garden".

Illegal Immigrants

This poem was written after I took a tour of the Little Bighorn Battlefield National Monument in Wyoming, the site of Custer's Last Stand.

It was the year eighteen sixty-eight.
The U.S. government signed the Fort Laramie Treaty.
The Black Hills were to be closed to white settlements,
Preserved for the Lakota Indians
Forever, so long as the buffalo roamed.

'Forever' lasted less than eight years.
The eastern railroads needed meat for their track crews,
So professional hunters followed the rails westward.
Men like 'Buffalo Bill' made their living
Killing the buffalo for meat, hides, and sport.

It was the year eighteen seventy-two.
America celebrated its centennial.
Gold was discovered in the Black Hills,
And people in their thousands rushed to the west
Seeking fortunes and living space.
Most of them were immigrants to America
Fleeing depression and prejudice,
And ready to ignore the letter of the treaty law.

Towns quickly sprung up along the immigrant trails.
Towns like Deadwood – an illegal encampment
In the midst of Indian land.
People like Calamity Jane – an illegal immigrant.
Wild Bill Hickok – another illegal.

In the year eighteen seventy-six
The U.S. government sent the army to remove the Indians
From 'their land'.
Almost half of Custer's troops
Were immigrants themselves
From seventeen different countries
And two marked down as 'unknown'.

You already know the basic story.
The Lakota won the battle
But lost the war and their sacred Black Hills.
General Custer became a legend,
The Indian culture was 'civilized',
And U.S. history moved on.

History is full of ironies.
Custer, a hero for the North side
Winning battles against slavery in the Civil War,
Won greater fame by dying in a war
To enslave the Lakota.
What's the lesson we should learn from all this?
Each of us standing here today is an 'illegal immigrant'.
We need to remember.

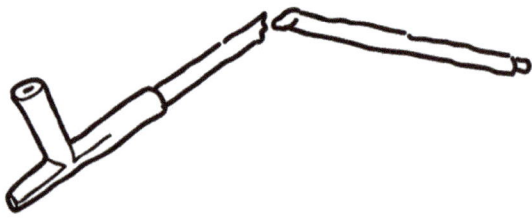

Ivan Stiles

Infinities Come In Sizes

Can you really understand the concept of a million years?
Is it really different in your mind from forever,
Days progressing into the future without end?

I have known people who lived past a hundred years.
It is a lifespan to which I greatly aspire.
My father was alive a hundred years ago,
And his memory is still fresh.

A thousand years ago is more problematic,
The stuff of history books and dusty museums
And ancient stories.
A thousand of these on end might as well be infinite.

In the 1880's, Georg Cantor made an amazing discovery.
Infinity is not a one-size-fits-all concept!
Some infinities are bigger than others – some infinitely larger!

Tell me the largest integer that there is –
"A hundred million billion trillion gazillion".
I'll just respond, "plus one".
We can play this game into forever,
Never reaching a limit based on just this
One simple generating rule.
Cantor called this a "countable infinity" – aleph 0.
Think of Biblical Abraham starting to count the stars.
He's still working on it.

Now, how many even integers are there?
You're tempted to think "half as many",
Since you've left out all the odd ones.
Yet, for every integer 'n' there is an even integer '2n'.
One simple generating rule again.
The even integers are countable, just like the regular integers,
And just like the odd integers too – '2n+1'.
Infinities can contain infinities.
But wait, it gets worse...

How many decimal numbers lie between 1 and 2?
There's 1.5 right in the middle.
We can generate other decimal numbers –
1.55, and 1.555 and 1.555 and ...
That's a countable infinity right there.
What about 1.05, 1.005, 1.0005 and ...
Another countable infinity.
We can create another similar infinity for every integer,
And with an infinity of generating rules,
An infinite number of infinities
In one small interval of the number line,
Like the whole world of life in a drop of pond water.
Cantor called this infinity size aleph 1.

You've heard of the mathematical term denoted 'pi',
The ratio of a circle's circumference to its diameter.
You might have recited "three point one four one five nine...".
Pi is a transcendental number.
It clearly lies between the integers 3 and 4,
Yet there is no known rule or pattern to its decimal digits.

Computers, both human and digital,
Have expanded pi to millions of digits
With no end or structure in sight.
There appear to be an infinite number
Of transcendental numbers.
Studded like stars along the number line.
You get a doctorate in mathematics if you can prove this.

I'm starting to get a headache.
This is supposed to be a poem,
Not a math lesson.

Creationists believe that the world was created in six days
About six thousand years ago.
A nice, comfortable, human, finite span of time
Readily conceived and understood.
Their concept of God constrained to a countable set.

My concept of God has to be larger
Than an unending stream of days.
Able to encompass many infinities, both even and odd.
Containing both fractions and transcendental values.
Like Cantor, we must see the worlds
Within worlds within worlds.
That's a God truly worthy of our worship.

Ivan Stiles

Christiana Wamsley

Kintsugi

Kintsugi (金継ぎ, "golden joinery"), also known as Kintsukuroi (金繕い, "golden repair"), is the Japanese art of repairing broken pottery by mending the areas of breakage with lacquer dusted or mixed with powdered gold, silver, or platinum, a method similar to 'Maki-e' technique. As a philosophy it treats breakage and repair as part of the history of an object, rather than something to disguise.

Kintsugi became closely associated with ceramic vessels used for 'chanoyu' (Japanese tea ceremony). One theory is that kintsugi may have originated when Japanese shogun Ashikaga Yoshimasa sent a damaged Chinese tea bowl back to China for repairs in the late 15th century. When it was returned, repaired with ugly metal staples, it may have prompted Japanese craftsmen to look for a more aesthetic means of repair. Collectors became so enamored of the new art that some were accused of deliberately smashing valuable pottery so it could be repaired with the golden seams of kintsugi.

Kintsugi can relate to the Japanese philosophy of "no mind" (無心 mushin), which encompasses the concepts of non-attachment, acceptance of change, and fate as aspects of human life.

"Not only is there no attempt to hide the damage, and the repair is literally illuminated... a kind of physical expression of the spirit of 'mushin'. 'Mushin' is often literally translated as "no mind," but carries connotations of fully existing within the moment, of non-attachment, of equanimity amid changing conditions The vicissitudes of existence over time, to which all humans are susceptible, could not be clearer than in the breaks, the knocks, and the shattering to which ceramic ware too is subject. This poignancy or aesthetic of existence has been known in

Japan as mono no aware, a compassionate sensitivity, or perhaps identification with, [things] outside oneself."

—Christy Bartlett, Flickwerk: "The Aesthetics of Mended Japanese Ceramics"

I am a flawed vessel.
Cracks show through the armor that I show to the world,
Chips and dents,
Gouges and scrapes,
From my 70 years of living.
Some parts of me show signs of wear,
And some parts have been replaced.

We live in a broken world.
Its surface fractured by real and artificial divisions.
Hundreds of national and personal boundaries
Scar its surface and burrow deep.
Some borders are natural
Shining rivers and wave-washed coastlines
Visible from high above.
Some borders are crater-marred war zones,
Retaining the memories of hurts and vengeances from long ago.
While some barbed wire edged borders mark mine fields
Killing zones of no-man's lands
As current as this evening's news report.

This poem, like its author, is imperfect.
It doesn't rhyme.
The rhythm of its words does not always flow
So smoothly as I'd like.
Not like the air and water flowing across the eroding edges
Of our unnecessary separations.

We are called to be the gold and silver dust…
In the lacquer that binds the broken parts together.
Remaking this pile of shattered pieces
Into a world of utmost beauty.

Ivan Stiles

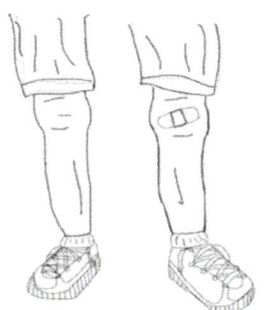

Christiana Wamsley

Leadership

The French aviator and writer Antoine de Saint-Exupéry was best known internationally as the author of "Le Petit Prince" ("The Little Prince"). Many self-help guides and books about management now contain a saying about motivation and organization that often has been attributed to Saint-Exupéry. Thanks to Carolyn Lesh, who brought this quotation to my attention.

If you wish to build a ship,
Do not divide your people into teams
And send them out to the forest
To cut wood.
Instead, teach them to long for the vast
And endless sea.

If you wish to build a country,
Do not divide your people into parties
And set them against each other
Seeking power.
Rather, inspire them to work together
For common goals.

Lumpy Gravy

I began to write this poem on the day before Thanksgiving. Can you tell?

Our universe began in a burst of light,
An explosion of total energy,
A "flash in the pan".

Expansion left it a sea of rarified gases,
Atoms floating in light-years of nothingness,
Like a tepid bowl of consommé.

Blobs of matter came to be,
Congealed like glistening fat
On a simmering pot.

Many eons of stirring later
Stars and planets arrived
As tiny specks in a vast tureen.

Today we live on one such ball of rock
A salt grain in the cosmic soup.
We owe our existence to a lump in the gravy.

Ivan Stiles

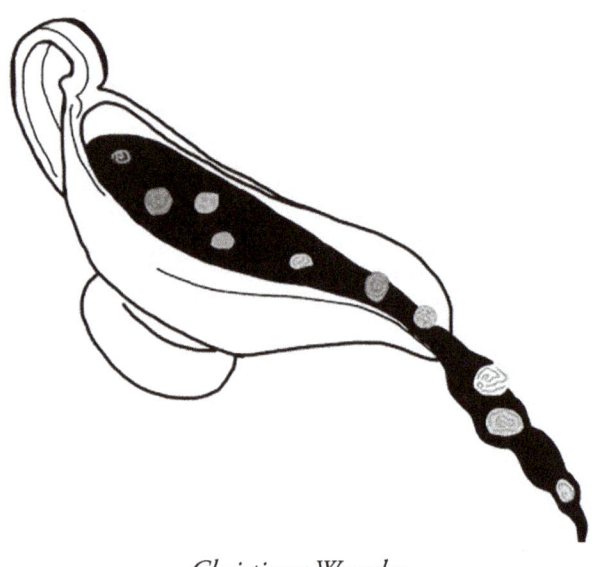

Christiana Wamsley

Maybe You Can

They say that you can't buy happiness,
That money alone doesn't bring peace.
Perhaps it can't,
But just maybe…

In 1922, Albert Einstein was staying at Tokyo's Imperial Hotel.
He'd just won the Nobel Prize in Physics.
A bellboy brought a message to his room,
And Einstein had no cash for a tip.

Einstein decided to tip in wisdom instead.
He wrote these words on hotel stationary
"A calm and modest life brings more happiness
Than the pursuit of success,
Combined with constant restlessness."
On a second sheet, he added
"Where there's a will, there's a way."

That bellboy was none too happy
Receiving philosophy instead of cash for a tip.
But, if he'd only kept those sheets of stationary…

In 2017 the first sheet sold at auction
For more than 1.5 million dollars,
And the second sheet for 250 thousand.
So, maybe you can indeed put a price
On the secret to happiness.
It's expensive!

Christiana Wamsley

Metallurgy

Purity.
For iron, that's not a desirable property.
Pure iron is soft and bends under pressure.
It rusts in the open air.
Pure iron cannot maintain a sharp edge.
It's the most-common element in the Earth.

Add 3 percent carbon and silicon to pure iron
And you get cast iron,
An alloy that's lightweight, stronger,
And more resistant to wear.

Add even more carbon to pure iron
And you get steel.
The foundation of modern industry
And construction, and transportation,
And weapons of war.

Add at least 10.5 percent of chromium to pure iron
And you get stainless steel.
Resistant to corrosion
And a good choice
For challenging environments.

Add nickel or tungsten to pure iron
And it's more resistant to high temperatures.
Add manganese for incredible durability.
Add vanadium to form Damascene steel,
Flexible yet tough,
Perfect for sword-making.

Purity.
For a society that's not a desirable property...
Too brittle and unable to adapt
When the environment changes.
Alloys and mixtures add needed strengths.
A pinch of spices add flavor to the dish.
Human societies need diversity
Like pure iron needs its additions.

Christiana Wamsley

My Coin Collection

When I was a boy I had a coin collection.
Each one a prime example of its type,
Worth well beyond the face value
Their small differences and minor flaws
Raising them in the eye of the collector.

In the beginning, God engraved a die with His image,
And stamped out Adam and Eve, the first 'proof set'.
Thousands of generations later
We're still made from that same original mold.
We each have the same face value – one human being,
But the Great Collector values us for our flaws,
And our differences.

Christiana Wamsley

My Own Kind

This poem came to me after I'd watched the new movie version of "West Side Story".

I am a man.
I am a white man.
I am an American white man.
I am a Jewish American white man.
My father came from Poland, and my mother came from Germany.
I am an Ashkenazic Jewish American white man.
I grew up in Ohio.
I am an Ashkenazic Jewish American white Buckeye man.
I graduated from the University of Michigan.
I am an Ashkenazic Jewish American white Buckeye
Wolverine man.
I have a beautiful wife.
I am an Ashkenazic Jewish American white Buckeye Wolverine
happily-married man.

This list of adjectives and categories is getting much too tedious and
cumbersome.
The distinctions are blurred and most overlap.
Let's just keep it simple.

I am a man.

Navajo Matzoh

Our tour group was served "Navajo Tacos" today for lunch. The base of the dish is a kind of fried bread that is a tradition among the Navajo people. The story behind this 'fry bread' reminded me of the unleavened bread (Matzoh in Hebrew) that Jews are commanded to eat during Passover to recall the hardships of Egyptian slavery,

In 1863, Kit Carson led the U.S. Army
Driving the Navajos from their ancestral lands
More than 300 miles away to Fort Sumner.
They called it "the Long Walk".

It all started in a dispute over the ownership of one horse,
Yet hundreds of Navajos died along the way
From starvation, disease, and bullets.
Many more would die in the holding camps
Until, four years later,
They were allowed to return home.

The Army gave the Navajos few provisions along the way.
The lard, flour, salt, sugar, baking powder and powdered milk
They did receive were often rancid.
Yet, from these poor ingredients they made
A food that would keep their people alive
Until the "Great Spirit" could lead them home.

Today, fry bread is a common food
Among many western Native American tribes.
To some, it is a sacred tradition,
To be eaten until the earth has, once again,
Been purified and all the people are free
And at peace.
It's a very familiar story.

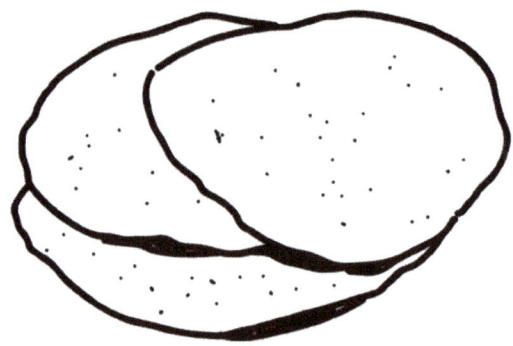

Ivan Stiles

Non-Trivial Zeros

The inspiration and title of this poem came to me from a line in the movie "Hidden Figures". The term itself comes from an area of advanced mathematics (the Riemann Zeta function) that investigates the mysterious distribution of prime numbers among the positive integers. The basic idea is that a mathematical function can have a 'standard' set of solutions (zeros) along with some more 'interesting' ones.

Sometimes I feel like a zero,
Totally worthless,
My life completely predictable,
Outcome changing nothing.

What changes a '1' to '100'?
Two zeros
Placeholders with a big impact
Almost nothing to everything.

Few of us can change the world,
Alter the flow of history,
And reverse the flowing tide.
Yet, each of us fills a place in God's plan
As a significant digit.

Opposite Sides of the Coin

This poem was inspired when I read Chapter 10 of the book "Humankind" written by Rutger Bregman. As a member of the human race, this book should be required reading.

Empathy.
"I feel your pain."
I shine a spotlight on your troubles.
You are important to me.
You are my focus.

Xenophobia.
My spotlight's bright, but it casts deep shadows.
Millions stand apart in the darkness.
I need to soften my focus,
And broaden the illumination.

What's nearby is easier to see,
While the distant is often hazy.
Close to us is naturally "close to us".
Difference is harder to discern.

But…everyone is close to someone,
And that someone is near to someone else.
Each lit place shines like a scattering of stars
While we wait for the sun to rise.

As the philosopher, Pogo, once said,
"We have met the enemy,
And they is us."

Pack It In, Pack It Out

I'm writing this poem in Bryce National Park. They say that you should always take out of the wilderness everything that you pack in. I'm not so sure!

I started on this trip with a load of expectations,
A bag full of misconceptions,
A suitcase of half-baked ideas,
And a backpack empty of first-hand knowledge.

I'm leaving with a satchel full of memories,
My misconceptions replaced by facts and stories.
My suitcase is full to bursting with wonderful images,
And the briefcase of my mind is filled with inspiration

Ivan Stiles

Paul's Letter to Conservatives

"When we think we have been hurt by someone in the past, we build up defenses to protect ourselves from being hurt in the future. So the fearful past causes a fearful future, and the past and future become one." <u>Alfred Hitchcock</u>

Memories of some early traumas are so clear in my mind,
They could have happened only yesterday.
Many cuts and bruises have shaped me.
Thick scabs formed over skinned knees
And bruised feelings.
Always on the lookout for dangerous chances,
I seek protection from any potential hurts.

In his first letter to the Corinthians
Paul wrote, "When I was a child,
I talked like a child,
I thought like a child,
I reasoned like a child.
When I became a man,
I set aside childish ways."

Like Paul,
We need to grow beyond our childhood memories.
We must venture out into the new and untried
Carefully, yet boldly,
With the assurance of youth
And the wisdom of maturity,
Neither scared of the unknown future
Nor scarred by our too well remembered past.
Mindful of history's lessons
Yet not forced to mindlessly repeat them.
This is the path to adulthood.

Political Discourse

I already know everything
Worth knowing.
If you agree,
I hear you!
If you don't agree
Then you're part of a great conspiracy,
Or deluded,
Or both.

Sometimes it's so funny
Just listening to your mistaken ideas.
They make for such great jokes.
I'm falling down, Laughing.

But,
You know,
That when we get up again,
Smiling at the joke,
At each other's 'alien' thought patterns,
It just might be
The beginning
Of a conversation.

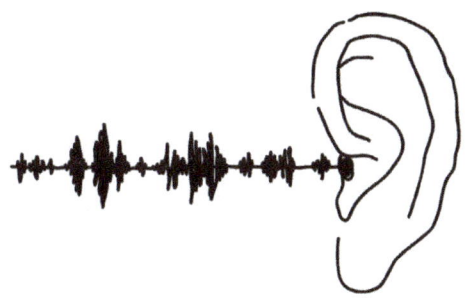

Ivan Stiles

Positive Glacial Dividend (PGD)

Thanks to Jon Wolkomir who told me about the PGD concept.

Is there anything that is totally good
Or completely bad,
Or – does every silver lining
Require a dark cloud?

The glaciers in Alaska are melting.
Feet of centuries-old ice
Disappear in weeks of global warming.
Torrents of once-trapped fresh water
Run along gravelly trenches.
New rivers become trout streams,
And water sources for growing towns.

The glaciers scoured miles of Alaskan land
Like a fleet of giant bulldozers.
Flecks of gold scraped and frozen in the ice.
Now the wealth runs with the water
And a new gold-rush begins.

There's just one problem with the PGD.
It's entirely short-term.
Once the dividend is spent,
It's gone forever…
Or – until the ice-age returns to Alaska
And the cycle repeats.

Purple Brains

This poem was derived from a TED talk video given by Hannah Holmes entitled "Red brain, blue brain — the neurobiology of political values". Her insightful talk covers everything from human biology to psychology to current-day politics. The illustrations come directly from her talk.

I am comfortable in my close circle of home.
It provides everything that I need.
My tribe has sufficient food and water.
Our population is stable.
I must protect my home from invasion.
This is how we evolved.
It's the way we've always lived.

But… there are things outside my home circle.
They could be nice too.
There is more food, more mating choices,
And some new technologies
For both tools and weapons.
Maybe I should consider them.
Maybe 'different' might be better.

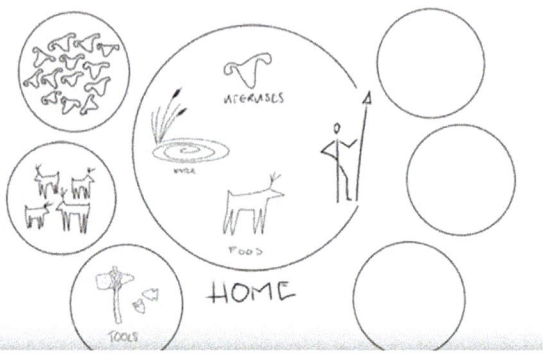

I'm afraid of new things.
The 'others' might not want to share with us.
There might be a war.
They might want to steal my food,
Or kidnap my people.
They might infect my tribe with their diseases.
It's safer to keep them out!

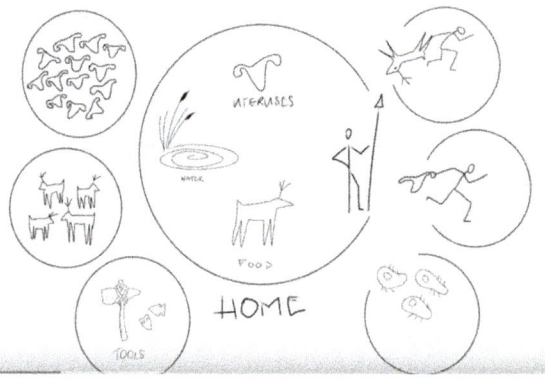

Two kinds of people evolved…
The 'welcomers', eager to expand and try new things
Even if they involve some degree of risk,
Who viewed the chances of growth as an opportunity,
And the 'shunners',
Averse to any kind of perceived danger
Before even trying out the 'new'.
Both types evolving alongside each other.
The 'red-brains' protecting the home circle,
And the 'blue-brains' expanding that circle.

One side of our brains evolved to see the dangers,
To intensely look out for looming pitfalls and traps,
To react quickly when feeling threatened.
The other side evolved to see the beautiful,
Regardless of the possible risks.
One side to say 'no' immediately
Until the other side has tried it for awhile
And it looks safe enough.

There's a balancing act
Constantly going on in our mammal brains.
Does the shiny new thing fit into our existing structure?
Can we stretch out our minds to encompass it?
Must we, instead, reject the 'new'
And just stick with what we already have?
Do we shout to the new and different "welcome in",
Or do we raise our spears
And rush to the city walls
Shouting "keep out"?

There is both good and bad in every change.
Evolution can provide new sources for love and companionship,
New food sources, cleaner water,
And technologies for better communication.
Changes in society might also bring less-satisfying work,
Tradition-defying medical and social choices,
And pandemics.

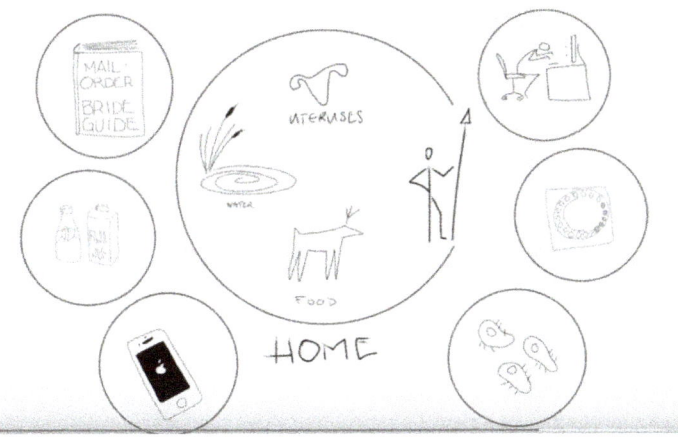

Each new entry into our circle of home
Might be an infector, or a staunch defender.
They might help us to harvest our food
Or they might take our jobs away.
They might be productive members of our tribe
Or they might just sap our resources.

The "red-brain" says 'better not risk it',
While the "blue-brain" says 'give them a chance'.
The "red-brain" likes order, structure, consistency,
And strong central leadership.
You need this for defense against outside threats.
When time is of the essence,
And immediate action is required.
The "blue-brain" likes lots of choices,
Variety, growth, and equality.
You need this to avoid stagnation.
The only issue is that all this choosing takes time.
The effects may not be seen immediately.
Deciding right and wrong takes lots of meetings.
Where all sides are expressed and weighed.

Evolution once filled the Earth with dinosaurs
Occupying every ecological niche.
Then, the environment changed
And we mammals evolved to take their places.
We evolved "red-brains" and "blue-brains"
In about equal percentages.
To survive, we need both types.
I guess that it's best for society
To be "purple-brained".

Putting Yourself Into The Picture

I'm standing at Artist's Point
Gazing out at the Lower Falls of the Yellowstone River
Three times higher than Niagara
Carving a magnificent multi-colored canyon
Across the landscape.

I'm peering through a picket fence of cellphones
As tourists take self-portraits
With the scenery as a mere backdrop.

Their pictures might last until their cellphones die
Or until the computers they were downloaded to
Grow obsolete.
Their printouts will become yellowing relics.
Their subjects might last eighty years or so.

This river has been flowing here for millennia.
The waterfall will outlast us all.
Now that's worthy of a photograph!

Ivan Stiles

Sankofa

Sankofa is an African word from the Akan tribe in Ghana. The literal translation of the word and the symbol is "it is not taboo to fetch what is at risk of being left behind." The sankofa symbolizes the Akan people's quest for knowledge among the Akan with the implication that the quest is based on critical examination, and intelligent and patient investigation. The symbol is based on a mythical bird with its feet firmly planted forward with its head turned backwards. Thus, the Akan believe the past serves as a guide for planning the future. To the Akan, it is this wisdom in learning from the past which ensures a strong future. The Akans believe that there must be movement and new learning as time passes. As this forward march proceeds, the knowledge of the past must never be forgotten.

A wise one is he who recalls the past,
Who takes to heart the lessons
That history teaches,
Who avoids the repetition
Of yesterday's failures,
Who knows that the latest wonder
Is so often just an old idea
Dressed in new clothes.

A wise one is she who walks forward
Towards a bright future full of promise,
Willing to explore the unknown
With a clear vision, and a little fear,
Who balances her past values
With her desired rewards,
Whose 'today' is always perched
Between 'yesterday' and 'tomorrow'.

Seventeen Camels

Sometimes mathematics can show the way to new and greater understandings.

There once was an old man who had seventeen camels.
He also had three sons.
His time was growing short,
So, the old man drew up his will.

"I leave half my herd to my eldest son, whom I love.
I then leave a third of my herd to my second son,
Whom I also love.
To my youngest son, who was always a scoundrel,
I leave one ninth of my herd."

The sons fell to arguing.
Their fighting was intense.
They could not obey their father's will.
Seventeen camels won't divide evenly by two,
Or by three, or by nine.
How could they honor their dear father's wishes?

The three sons went to see a wise old woman in their village.
She thought about their problem for a long while.
She said, "I don't know if I can help you,
But, if you want, you can have my camel too."

The eldest son took nine camels,
Half of the herd of eighteen,
And departed.

The second son took six camels,
One third of the herd,
And departed.

The youngest son saw that three camels were left.
"I am only entitled to one ninth of my father's herd…
Two camels."

The youngest son recognized the wisdom of the old woman.
He returned her camel to her,
And departed the village in peace.

Ivan Stiles

Silence is Consent

I used to be a U.S. delegate to the International Civil Aviation Organization (ICAO) – a branch of the United Nations dealing with air-traffic control technology. We had a rule in our meetings and deliberations that "silence is consent" for any vote.

This poem came to me while visiting an exhibit describing the treatment of interned American citizens of Japanese descent during the Second World War.

Not to decide is to decide –
Apathy is equivalent to agreement.
Failure to dissent means tacit approval.
Tolerance of evil marks complicity with the act.

Turning a blind eye does not make the sight disappear.
Blocking one's ears does not counteract the cries,
Nor does empty silence not echo with meaning.

Saying "it's not my concern",
Really means "I don't care enough to say 'no' ",
You don't have the option to simply vote "present".

Choose to speak.

Ivan Stiles

Six Philosophies

Close your eyes.
Imagine a perfect circle.
Now, try to draw one.
Most of us can conceive perfection,
But none of us will ever achieve it.
That's Plato's metaphysics.

"I think, therefore I am."
Our senses aren't all that's real.
The fact that you can doubt everything,
Including your own existence,
Is Descartes' proof that you do exist.

There is no 'divine right' for kings to rule.
How to build a strong state,
While preserving individual freedoms,
Was the central problem of the day.
(It still is!)
Rousseau's solution was the "general will".

Before Schopenhauer,
Art was just a frivolous diversion,
Not an expression of our innermost feelings.
Held captive by our wills, strivings, and desires,
We were doomed to suffering.
Schopenhauer said that art functions to free us.
A quasi-religious experience,
Instead of mere craftsmanship.

Nietzsche wrote "God is dead."
At least, He did not rule 19th century Europe.
People could fall into despair,
Or seek new "religions" elsewhere.
Nietzsche shuddered at that second option.
He proposed that people rise above
Conventional morality
To create new values celebrating
The beauty and suffering of existence.

Remember Plato's ideal forms?
That everything we see is but an imitation
Of a perfection not possible to achieve.
Sartre said that essences do not pre-exist people.
We are not some imperfect manifestation
Of some great cosmic blueprint.
We are not "condemned to be free".
"Life is nothing until it is lived.
The value of it is nothing else
But the sense that you choose."

Socialism and Stability

"Intellectuals start revolutions, but barbarians end them."

I have a magic wand.
If you will vote for me, I promise
That, on the day of my inauguration,
I will wave my wand,
And every person in our country,
Will be exactly equal,
The same bank balance,
And the same debts.
Each job will pay the same
And all will owe the same taxes.

Weeks and months pass…
Some will suffer accidents,
Financial reverses, and poor choices.
Some will be luckier and some work harder.
Some strive to a better life for all
While others yield to gratification of self
And squander what equality has given them.

In four years of time
I must wave my wand again
I must restore the balance and even the score.
Yet again, some will surge ahead
And others fall behind
By luck or accident – talent or laziness,
Chance or greater effort.

Again, the people will call for me.
"Forget about elections.
Just keep waving your wand!"
I will cease to be called 'president'
And I will become your dictator
As you yield up your freedom
For stability.

That's the problem with most "isms".
They're never stable.
They start out wonderfully
Then dissolve back into the chaos
From which they sprang.
The elite and the poor are always with us.
They just change names.

We long for conflicting goals.
We want stability and predictability
But we cannot tolerate stagnation.
We want freedom,
Room to grow, expand, create, improve,
While recognizing our fear of newness
And the unknown future.
We seek peace and an end to war.
We want to keep all that we have,
But…what you have looks nice too,
And you might not let me have it,
If I just ask nicely.

There are no magical wands.
No one can promise both ends
From our set of desirable choices.
We must juggle our desires
To achieve an equitable balance.
It's the best anyone can do.

Ivan Stiles

Spiritual Defibrillator

During the Jewish High Holidays, the congregation recites a long list of sins that might have been committed by someone in the community. It is a tradition that we beat our fist against our chest after each poten- tial sin is read. Thank you, Rabbi Mike, for the title and the images in this poem.

Well, God,
It has been another year
And I'm still here.
Thank You!

My soul is really tired though,
My spirit dull and lifeless,
My heart is empty and uninspired,
In need of resuscitation.

Then comes a knock on the door,
A wake-up call,
A shock of awakening,
A cry of alarm.

I'm alive again, God.
Thank You for the spark.
Thank You for the new beginning.
Thank You for my life.

Ten Righteous Ones

The Lord God said,
"The outcry against Sodom and Gomorrah is very great.
Their sins are so terrible.
Their transgressions are so profound.
I may have to destroy these places."

But Abraham said,
"Will You really sweep away the good with the wicked?
Will You not spare these cities
For the sake of fifty righteous ones?
Will not the Supreme Judge of all the earth do justly?"
The Lord said, "If I can find fifty righteous ones within the cities,
I will spare the whole place on their account."

But Abraham said,
"Suppose the fifty righteous ones lack but five.
Will You really destroy the cities for the lack of five?"
God replied, "If I find forty-five there, I will not destroy them."

The Book of Genesis describes how this bargaining went on...
Forty, thirty-five, thirty,
Twenty-five, twenty, fifteen... Finally, Abraham said,
"Suppose only ten righteous ones can be found there?"
And the Lord answered,
"For the sake of these ten, I will not destroy them."

The U.S. Senate has 100 members,
Two from each state, red and blue,
Today equally divided,
Fifty Republicans,
Fifty Democrats.
To take any significant action,
To avoid a filibuster requires sixty votes,
Ten Senators must forsake their party affiliation
And act for the good of the nation,
Like the ten righteous ones
Who could have saved Sodom and Gomorrah.

Ivan Stiles

The Bomber Fallacy

This poem came to me while I was thinking about the 'Bomber Fallacy' – an example of the psychological concept known as 'survivorship bias'. We tend to incorrectly evaluate situations based on the limited set of examples we choose to consider.

During World War II, researchers from the Center for Naval Analyses conducted a study on the damage done to returned aircraft after missions. They recommended adding armor to the areas that showed the most damage in order to minimize bomber losses to enemy fire. However, Abraham Wald suggested differently.

Wald was a Hungarian mathematician and a member of the Statistical Research Group (SRG), where he applied his statistical skills to vari- ous wartime problems. He noted that the study was only conducted on the aircraft that had survived their missions. It didn't paint a complete picture when the bombers that had been shot down were not presented for the damage assessment.

With that, the holes in the returning aircraft were areas that need no extra armor — since the bombers could take damage and still return safely. On the other hand, the areas where the returning aircraft were unscathed are those areas that, if hit, would cause the plane to crash and be lost. Wald then proposed that the Navy reinforce areas by adding more armor to them which was a perfect demonstration of how to not fall prey into the survivorship bias.

> Popular wisdom suggests:
> Emulate famous achievers.
> Bill Gates and Steve Jobs were college dropouts,
> So I'm not going to my classes today.

Popular wisdom suggests:
Emulate the rich.
Consider the winners in life's lottery.
Ignore the millions of losers
Who never get a moment's notoriety.

Popular wisdom suggests:
Only the 'exceptional' are worthy of our notice.
The 'normal' are, by definition,
The standard by which all are judged.
Even the best baseball batter fails two-out-of-three.
We should praise all those who get into the game.

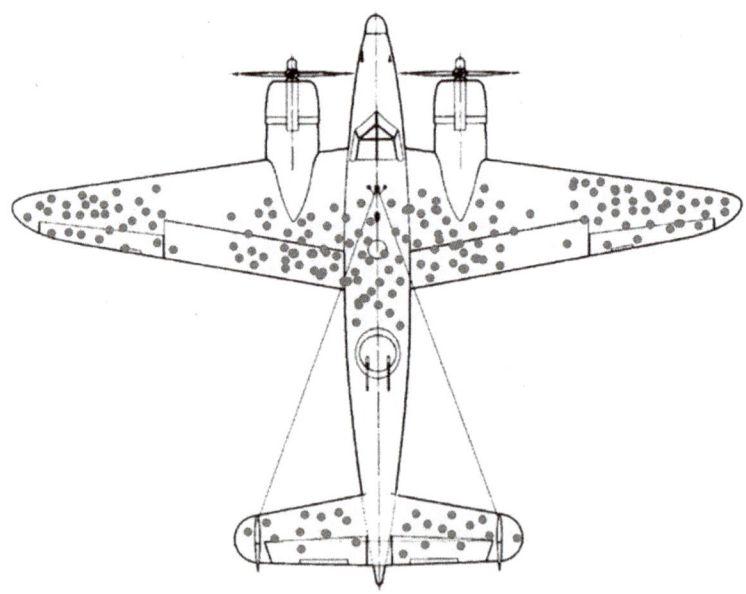

The Divine Ledger

The Jewish High Holiday liturgy contains an image of God as the great supernatural accountant sitting before a ledger book where the fates of each living creature are recorded. I picture God pausing, pen in hand, about to write in my entry for this year. We are told that prayer, righteousness, and deeds of kindness can "avert the severity of the decree".

I was born with a number of handicaps:
My mother's myopia, and Dad's hairline,
Mom's high blood pressure,
My father's sleep apnea,
And a human being's mortality.

Surgery has improved my sight.
One pill each day keeps my blood pressure down.
A CPAP machine cured my snoring.
I'll just live with the baldness,
But nothing cures the mortality.

So, I will try to get more exercise,
And watch my diet better.
I will reduce my stress level,
And take more walks in the sun.
I will love my wife and the times we share.
I will be more attentive to others' needs
And seek to help whenever I can.

It won't cure the mortality, But it can't hurt!

Ivan Stiles

The Enemy of Progress

The primary ideas in this poem derive from past episodes of the television program "Mythbusters" on the Science Channel.

I once saw a billboard that read,
"Tradition is the enemy of progress".
This seems wrong on so many levels.

The word 'enemy' implies a "them or us" mentality.
More of one must mean less of the other,
They cannot coexist.
One must be 'bad' and the other inherently 'good'.
Why not a balance – opposite sides of a single coin?

Did you ever try to walk blindfolded,
Across a trackless field with no landmarks,
With nothing to guide you – no visible destination?
You'll find that it's just about impossible.
Your path quickly becomes a 'random walk',
Wandering off course or doubling back.
There'll be plenty of meandering distance covered,
But no discernable goal achieved.
You just keep walking aimlessly in that open field.

Imagine that you are behind the wheel of a car,
But you are blindfolded.
You cannot see the road ahead, or any obstacles in your path.
Do you think you could drive safely this way?
"Not too likely", you say –
An accident waiting to happen.

Suppose you have a co-pilot sitting in your car's passenger seat,
Able to give you instructions, when to turn
And when to stop,
Warning of dangers in advance and keeping you aware.
Do you think you could drive safely now?
It turns out this tandem driving technique works pretty well.
Like the pilot of a plane in stormy weather,
Relying on instruments, checklists, and procedures,
You can reach your destination

'Progress' means going forward – but which way is 'forward'?
Without landmarks and history, how do you guide your steps?
If you don't remember where you've been,
How will you recognize that you've doubled back,
Retracing well-worn steps that led to nowhere?

'Tradition' tells us about where we started from,
Where we are today,
And where we'd like to go tomorrow.
It tells us about times when we wandered off the chosen path,
And what destinations are worth going toward.

'Progress' is the urge to be moving and growing.
'Tradition' is the guide and director of our steps.
Clearly, we need both in balanced measure
Not wandering blindly through an unseen field,
But driving with a wise co-pilot by our side.

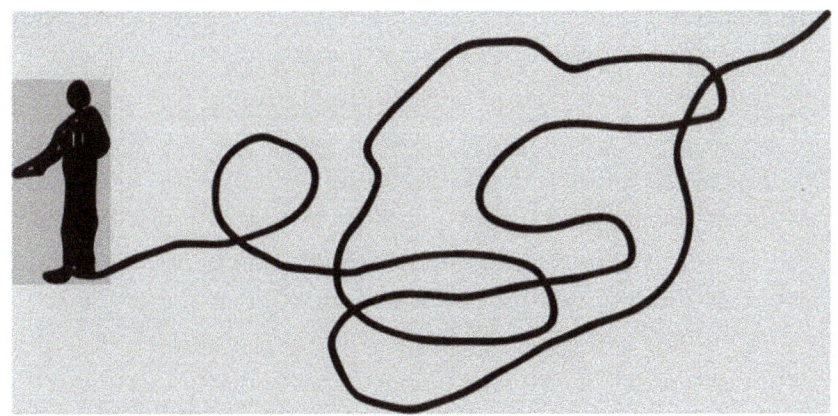

Ivan Stiles

The Fig Tree and Health Care

An issue on many people's minds today is how national health care should be funded. Is it just too expensive? Should everyone have to carry a federally mandated level of insurance? Should people have the option of not paying for insurance until they actually need it? I'm reminded of a story from ancient Rabbinic lore…

A gray old man stoops beside a dusty road
Digging a hole in the earth outside a small village.
He plants a fig seed beside a long row of trees,
And waters the seed from his heavy bucket.

A young man is travelling down the road towards town
Stops to talk to the old man as he finishes planting.
"Do you really expect to eat the figs from that tree?"
"No", the old man replied, "probably not".

"This row of trees bore fruit when I was just a boy.
My grandfather planted the oldest ones here,
And my father planted the second row in the grove.
I've been eating their figs all my life."

"No, I'm planting this tree for my children.
They'll eat its fruit and remember me when I'm gone."
The old man stood, brushed the dust from his pants,
And both men walked down the road together.

A young man thinks, "I'm really healthy today.
Why should I pay for insurance that I won't need now?
It's so much money that I could spend on other things.
I'll worry about my health when I'm a lot older!"

"I could pay down some of my student loans
Or take a year off to travel in Europe.
I could live with my parents for another year
And have a down payment on a nice new car."

An old man thinks, "I can't afford to pay for all my medicine,
And my wife can't get the operation she needs so badly.
Maybe an insurance plan would have been a good investment.
My kids shouldn't have to watch their parents die too soon."

The Gisters

The proposed bill runs to over 300 pages,
Almost a thousand paragraphs,
Filled with whereas' and wherefores',
Dependent clauses and multiple exceptions,
Definitions of terms and multiple footnotes,
Dizzying even to a lawyer.

The Senator's staff pores over the material for many days,
Extracting the significant concepts from the welter of detail,
Seeking clarity from the morass of 'legalese'.
They draft a 20-page summary memo,
With, hopefully, just the pertinent points.

The Senator's chief aide
Reads through the staff's summary memo
And jots down a few bullet points.
He considers the political implications
And the polling numbers,
And writes a one-page statement
For the Senator to read.

The Senator scans the one-page summary.
He mainly reads just the bullet sentences.
He's not so interested in all the details and loopholes,
He's more interested in how his donors will be impacted,
And how his vote will affect his political base.

In the end, the bill's hundreds of pages,
Its legal definitions and details,
The work, hopes, ideas, and dreams,
Of many interested people
Boil down to just one word for the Senator…
Vote "yes" or "no".

Ivan Stiles

The Incompleteness Proof

God, the master craftsman,
Set out to build this world.
At the end of each workday
He'd hang up his tool belt,
Clean up the job-site,
Stand back and say to Himself,
"It looks good".

The end of the project was at hand.
God said, "that was a hard week's work.
I think I'll rest for a while,
And turn things over to humanity,
For maintenance."

If I were selecting a contractor
To renovate my house,
I'd expect better references than
"He does good work",
And I'd expect him to have completed
More than one job.

God didn't give us a perfect world
On purpose.
He left us room to perfect the design,
To add trim and wallpaper,
Modernize the appliances,
And add rooms as our families grow.

We start with a firm foundation,
True walls, and a tight roof.
It's up to us now,
To maintain the plumbing,
(The water pure and flowing).
Replace the A/C filters,
(The air free of contamination).
Keep the refrigerator stocked
(So, no one need starve).
And work to finish the job
"Perfectly".

Ivan Stiles

The Mark of Insanity

Albert Einstein is supposed to have said that the mark of insanity is to perform the same behavior repeatedly while expecting a different outcome each time.

Medieval London was wreathed in a smoky cloud
As coal replaced wood-burning fireplaces.
The verdant English forests were long since gone.
It was the thirteenth century
And Londoners knew the stench of many lime kilns.
The poor of the city breathed the poisoned air
While the rich moved outward to the yet unspoiled countryside.

It was the 1940's and our country was at war.
Newly built steel mills in Warren, Ohio belched fire and slag
Into the gray clouds that hung over my hometown.
The winter snow had a rusty tinge,
And the rain was tinted like diluted blood.
We won the war – but the pollution still remains.

It was December fifth of 1952,
And the "Big Smoke" descended on London.
In four days of blinding fog,
More than four thousand people died
From breathing in the results of too many coal fires
And a stagnant weather pattern.
New studies think the death toll might have been nearly 12,000.
Ambulances couldn't go out to collect the dead
When the streets were too dark to travel on,
And those who were able
Purchased "smog masks" from the chemist shops.

Researchers say that at least 366,000 people
Died prematurely in 2013
In China – the result of industrial coal burning.
Tourists on the streets of Beijing wear breathing masks
While China burns more coal
Than the rest of the world combined.
Chinese industry booms – killing more people every year
Than dirty water and lack of sanitation in poorer countries.

Our country's leader tells us
We must preserve the nation's coal industry.
These jobs are far more important than "global warming".
Do we expect the outcome to change this time around?

Ivan Stiles

The Sins of the Fathers

This poem was inspired while thinking about the unfortunate, but widely held, belief that COVID-19 vaccines are made from aborted fetuses, and that taking the vaccine makes one complicit with those who perform abortions.

In 1973, a woman in Holland had an abortion.
Supposedly therapeutic in nature,
But that's irrelevant to this poet.
Cells from her baby's kidney tissue
Were treated in a laboratory
With adenovirus type 5
And the HEK 293 cell line was born.

Jump ahead more than 45 years.
That's hundreds of generations of cloned cells.
No doctors or operations involved,
Just Petri dishes and some biochemistry.

HEK 293 cells purchased from laboratory supply
Were used to develop and test
Potential COVID-19 vaccines.
Many tens of thousands of lives saved
And many more each day,
Because of this one life lost.

That's the true miracle in all of this.
One life lost so long ago – one original 'sin'
Transformed into the savior for so many.
So much good throughout the world…
What an amazing legacy.

Christiana Wamsley

The Smell Of Gunpowder

This poem was written just after the 50th anniversary of the Apollo 11 first moon landing—a momentous event in human history and in this poet's lifetime.

Many of the Apollo astronauts commented that
Moon dust smells just like burnt gunpowder.
They should know.
All but two of them were military men
Who could recall the odor of firearms and bullets.

The rockets they rode on
Were barely-controlled bombs,
The end products of wartime research
For vengeance weapons.

The impetus that drove NASA to the moon
Was fear of a Cold War with Russia
Escalating into nuclear holocaust.
Thankfully, we went to the moon instead.

Ivan Stiles

The Unexpected Pleasure of Rituals

*This poem was inspired when I read an article written by Leah Fessler
in the November 11, 2019 issue of the New York Times. While we seek
new experiences, we often fail to notice, appreciate, and enjoy aspects of
the familiar that we've missed.*

My mind is constantly bombarded with stimuli,
Sights, sounds, smells, and feelings
Accost me from every side.
The tickle of a fresh spring breeze against my face,
The itch of a new flannel shirt,
A fleeting memory of my first love,
And the remembered scent of my mother's kitchen
When she was baking strudel.

How can I concentrate on the song of a bird
Or notice the graceful curl of a fern
While watching out for roots and stones
Along a forest path?
I lack enough consciousness to process it all.
I've got to filter most of the inputs away,
Actually noticing only a fraction of what is there.
Each experience is seen only through the limits I impose.

We've evolved to pay attention to the new and flashy things
That might prove dangerous or exciting.
We discount the familiar,
The "been-there-and-done-that" stuff.
Yet, there is newness in what I choose to see,
What I select from the parade of images
Which confront my eyes,
Each experience seen in a new way.

There is a chance for pleasure in repetition,
An opportunity for richness and expanded joy
When the commonplace has been stripped away.
We assume too quickly that we've seen
"All there is to see"
When, in fact, we've only scratched the surfaces.
There are always nuances, new insights,
And new inspirations.
Your favorite food will never taste so good
As when you haven't had it for a month.

Life's rituals can be like one vast Thanksgiving table
Where the platters and the plates are comfortably familiar.
Yes, there is the turkey and the gravy,
But the cranberry sauce is a new recipe,
And who brought those new dinner rolls?
The wine we drink is always a new vintage,
Even though the glasses are the same as last year.
We bring the "newness" to the table with us.

Ivan Stiles

The Valley of Despair

This poem is based on the psychological theory known as the Dunning-Kruger Effect. As a person starts out to learn any new thing (playing an instrument, writing poetry, etc.) there comes an initial euphoria where one underestimates the difficulty of the thing while simultaneously over-estimating one's ability to do the thing. As one continues to learn, the initial euphoria is replaced by a feeling of despair that the task is too hard and one's ability too limited. Only then, for those few who persevere beyond the despair, comes the renewed joy of true knowledge.

A little knowledge
Is a dangerous thing.
I don't know
What I don't know.
I'm a really big fish
In my small pond.

Suddenly, the dam breaks.
My comfortable pond
Pours out into a vast ocean.
Tiny ripples turn into towering waves.
I must keep swimming
Although I cannot see the shore.

I'm so tired.
My progress seems so limited.
Each stroke brings me no further,
No closer to that imagined sunlit island
Somewhere – out there
Beyond my limited view.

Until, one day
I raise my view
And see the shining sand and the palm trees.
Achievement must be earned
By a lot of paddling against the wind.
The shore is a beautiful sight.

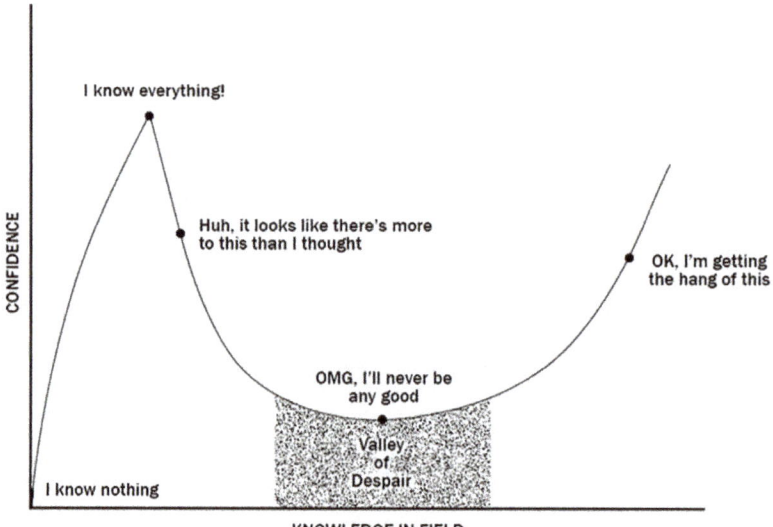

The World's Finest Camera

True, my camera doesn't have
The spectral range of some specialized ones.
It doesn't register ultraviolet, except for an occasional sunburn,
And it only senses infrared as the sun's warmth on my face.

My camera has a wide-angle view.
It doesn't require a tripod,
And it always records 3-D images in full color.

My camera weighs next to nothing,
And it's always with me.
I can't lose it, or leave it behind.

My camera is always in video mode.
It has sufficient storage for a lifetime
Of beautiful pictures and memories.

My camera is my eye,
The download is my brain and heart.
My camera is always fully charged.

Tradition and Darwin

This poem contrasts the codification of traditions with the growth of species through the metaphor of the Passover Seder plate. Researching this topic brought out lots of very interesting variations on the symbolic foods of the Seder.

Try to do something once.
It's a chance event, a mutation.
That might die away without a trace.
But if a thing has value and improves the world
It might live on to a third attempt.
"Third time's a charm" the saying goes,
When simple luck becomes a tradition.

Consider the chain of traditions
On the Passover Seder plate.
At least six symbolic foods
To remind us of our history
And our treasured values
Each with a back-story evolved over time.

What about the roasted shank bone?
Are we all still shepherds?
Does lamb remind us of wealth and ease?
But if you haven't got a flock of sheep
Maybe you have a flock of chickens.
A chicken neck becomes the symbol
Of ample food in a world with no poverty,
"A chicken in every pot".
But what if you're a vegetarian?
The great eleventh century Rabbi, Rashi said
Use a beet instead – red as animal blood.

A roasted egg, so our tradition says,
Symbolizes the festival sacrifice
Once offered in the ancient Temple.
But…that sacrifice was actually a lamb,
And the Temple is a distant memory.
Which came first,
The tradition or the symbol?
Does it remind us of the first meal of a mourner,
Dipped in salt water to remind us of tears,
Or in vinegar – a reminder of the bitterness
Of slavery in every generation?

Matzos – the "bread of affliction"
We're commanded to eat on Passover
As a reminder of the exodus from Egypt.
As a symbol it comes in triples:
Three Matzos on the Seder plate,
Three groupings of our people
(Conductors, Singers, and Listeners),
Three measures of flour that Sarah baked
When visited by three angels.
It takes three times to mark a tradition.

Fresh green vegetables remind us of Spring,
The season of new growth and rebirth.
"Let all who are hungry come and eat."
But if your land is late to produce,
If your climate is colder than Israel at Passover time,
Make a symbol of what you do have
Perhaps a potato.

Bitter herbs on the Seder plate,
(My tradition uses horseradish),
Remind us of the bitterness felt in oppression.
Some people use romaine lettuce instead.
Its leaves are not bitter themselves
But the root turns hard and bitter
When left too long in the ground.
Like Pharaoh who was at first a friend to Joseph
But then his heart was hardened.

Charoseth – symbolic of the mortar
Our Israelite ancestors used to build
Great cities for Pharaoh.
Google lists more than 130 thousand recipes for Charoseth
Each one a local tradition,
Each one with local additions and 'special' ingredients,
Like stone dust in Gibralter.
Yet, isn't it ironic that,
After decades of careful research and analysis,
Modern scientists cannot agree
On the formula for Egyptian mortar
Either.

When half of this world's population
Is considered inferior on the basis on their gender
And valued only for procreation.
Such a sad waste of human resources
That it's worthy of a new symbol to remind us.
Hence, the orange on the Seder plate.
As likely as a woman Rabbi, it was once said.
As likely as the Hebrews escaping from mighty Egypt
While Moses' sister, Miriam,
Sang a song at the shore of the sea.

Today we need to recall the unrest in our world.
Where there is hatred and destruction
Instead of growth and understanding.
We need to plant olive groves
Instead of burning forests.
We should strive to add to the human condition
Rather than building fences around our fields.
So…olives were added to the Seder plate.

Traditions must be living things
Growing and changing with their time and place,
What is important today,
What we need to remember.
For when a tradition hardens into stone
And refuses to grow and encompass the new,
It becomes a fossil,
Only worthy of a dusty shelf In a museum.

Uniforms

We all wear uniforms – outward signs of who we are inside. The import-ant thing to remember is that we can always go home and change our clothes.

A police officer wears his black shirt
With silver rank insignias and brass buttons
The black man wears his dark skin
Adorned with gold chains and a Rolex.

On Sunday, the policeman wears a white shirt
With a red striped tie and a blue suit to church.
While the black man sports a white tuxedo
And celebrates the wedding of his daughter.

The ER nurse wears a starched white uniform
With comfortable soft white shoes.
The next day she wears a "little black dress"
And goes out to a dance club to 'party'.

The cop's black shirt and the bride's white gown
The gold chains and the red striped tie…
We each wear a uniform of the day
That we show to the world outside.

We get to try on many colors
It's never just black or white.

Utepils

You have to live through the long dark months of a Norwegian winter to appreciate the annual Norwegian rite of utepils. Literally it means "the first drink of the year taken out of doors". Easter is barely past, with its tradition of hyttepåske – your Easter visit to your remote cabin – and the days are at last getting longer. Although it's still practically freezing, everyone is queueing up to invite you to a first utepils get-together at their favorite bar.'

Actually, the word utepils simply means any beer enjoyed outside, at any time of the year, but it is true that the first one of the season is a much-anticipated ritual. You know that spring is on its way when Norwegians brave the chilling temperatures and gather around their pints, sometimes even wrapped in blankets. The practice continues throughout the year though – nothing says summer like utepils.

The word itself is made up of two words, ute ('outside') and pils, which is simply short for Pilsner, the type of lager beer most commonly consumed in Norway. Interestingly, pils is also used as a slang verb ('å pilse'), meaning simply 'to drink beer'. So, when you are getting together for an utepils you are pilsing.

It has been a long, cold winter,
A year of social-distancing,
Each of us huddled behind our walls
Pierced only by the light of computer screens
And dear voices over telephones.

It has been a long, cold winter
A year without gatherings,
Each of us hearing only our own music
Celebrating virtual rites in quiet loneliness
Inside our own souls.

It has been a long, cold winter
But we sense that Spring is coming
As we receive our vaccinations
To boost our personal immunities
And warm our souls.

It has been a long, cold winter
But now the sun is rising.
The days are growing longer
And joys become easier to find.
Summer is nearing.

It has been a long, cold winter,
But even a frozen river thaws in time.
We will share new times together.
We will play new songs in harmonious chorus.
We will smile again.

Let us praise the ending of a long, cold winter.
Let us raise a glass to the greening of Spring.
Let us drink a health to the rebirth of life,
The start of a new season with song and story.
It was a long, cold winter.

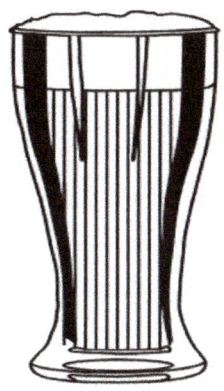

Ivan Stiles

Christiana Wamsley

Walking On A Teapot

People who say, "it's as solid as a rock"
Never visited Yellowstone.
Here the rocks lift and crack,
Bulge and recede,
Turn to liquid and then reform.
Water roils and boils,
Steams and bubbles,
Surges and splashes
All in a very human timescale.

Yellowstone lies atop a super volcano,
Tens of miles across,
So large that its rim lies beyond the horizon
Like a giant stove cooking the lakes and streams
While we tourists hike along the rattling teapot lid.

Now, where did I put my teabag?

Ivan Stiles

WD-40

Sometimes even the most mundane things can have interesting history behind them. Even a commercial trademark can leave a wonderful trail. Thanks to Lorraine Stalians, our tour guide through the U.S. National Parks, who brought this history to my attention.

It was 1958, in the heat of the Cold War.
The U.S. Air Force needed a protective coating
For its new Atlas ballistic missile.
A rocket so flimsy that it had to be inflated
Lest it collapse in a ball of flame on the launch-pad,
Or when the world would collapse in a sea of fire
Soon after the launching.

Three men from South Dakota took on the challenge.
They developed a formula.
It failed.
They tried again with renewed hope.
It failed.
Thirty-nine times they tried, and failed,
But, the fortieth formula worked
And the threat of the Atlas missile
Kept the peace for over a decade.

They called it "Water Dispersant Formula 40".
(It could also have meant "Weapon of Destruction",
But no matter.)
The Atlas missile was never fired in anger.
It launched the Mercury astronauts into space instead.

We haven't beaten our swords into plowshares
Or our spears into pruning hooks.
We did transform a piece of atomic warfare technology
Into the universal lubricant,
Able to fix a rusty hinge and silence a squeaky door.
Not bad for the first try.

What Is Love?

This poem is dedicated to my wonderful wife of 38 years. In this weird limbo-world of pandemic, it is the best I can do in the anniversary-present department.

One word,
Four letters,
One syllable,
Two people,
One lifetime shared.

One square dance,
Forty years we've known
Since that night,
Time spent growing ever closer,
Experiences shared.

Two families
Two circles of friends become one.
Two hearts, linked in rhythm.
Joys made brighter
Sorrows eased.

Happy Anniversary
My dearest Lynda.
My one enduring present.

Yellow Purse

Believe it or not, this poem/song parody was written during an MRI exam. My wife, Lynda, had been shopping for a yellow handbag. The tune is 'borrowed' from the old calypso song "Yellow Bird".

Yellow purse, high up there on the shelf.
Yellow purse, I want you for myself.
You're made of plastic, and…
You have elastic, and…
I hold you in my hand…
I think you look just grand…
And when I get you home…
Pile in everything I own…
Oh, how I'll love my new purse.

Yellow purse, they want me to pay full price.
Yellow purse, I don't think that's very nice.
I shop from store to store…
Each one is charging more…
Drive all around the town…
Waiting for your mark-down…
Then one day I read…
Exactly what I need…
They've finally put you on sale.

Yellow bag — you'll carry all my swag.
Yellow bag — you clean up with just a damp rag.
I went shopping every day…
I even put some on lay-away…
But when the day was done…
I knew they were not the one…
Then, finally, one night…
This one's exactly right…
I've just found my new bag.

My pink pants, I think they were made in France.
My pink pants, I wear them at every chance.
They go with my new shirt…
A necklace wouldn't hurt…
They're just my favorite shade…
I got them tailor-made…
There's just one thing I fear…
That always brings a tear…
They just don't go with my purse.

Your Fist, My Nose

First-order freedoms:
To walk wherever I want
Whenever I want to.
To think what I want
To say what I think.
To swing my arms in a free and easy stride
Down the sidewalk of my life.
To wear a COVID mask if I choose
And get the shot – or not.

Second-order freedoms:
To walk unafraid
Of bumps and bruises
Trips and falls
My first-order freedoms unmolested
And my quiet strolls uninterrupted
By the shouts of others.

When freedoms intersect
In human interactions large and small
Where our personal liberties conflict
A compromise is required.

Your first-order freedom to swing your fist
Ends
Where my second-order nose
Begins.

Ivan Stiles